VIN

"Still Here
By Margot Harris

CONTENTS

ABOUT THE AUTHOR

After an active life, this first-time author thought it would be worthwhile to share eight decades of how she has experienced the world in the hope that you will find the experience of reading it as entertaining, insightful and educational as she found the process of writing it cathartic. Margot Harris (b.1930) currently lives in Maidenhead with her husband Henry and works as a counsellor for her own private practice, Fusion Counselling.

Definition of Memoir
"A memoir is how one remembers one's own life."

DEDICATION

To my husband Henry who has helped me to put down the roots that allowed me to reach my potential; to all my wonderful friends who have been a continuous source of inspiration; to my professional colleagues; and my thanks to all the clients that I have had the privilege of meeting over the years, who have trusted me and taught me so much about the human condition.

AMAZON EDITION

Published by Frosty Grape Publishing

Cover Design by Melissa@ SweetberryDesign.co.uk
Edited by Sebastian K Gach

Website: http://www.vintage1930.co.uk

PROLOGUE

I like to think that like a good wine I have matured with age, but that like the grape I have had to survive my fair share of frosty moments. Yet,

… **Still here**!

A life lasting eighty years is a long, sometimes arduous and yet, more often than not, enjoyable journey. When we are young, a week can seem like a long time. During our childhood, we cannot begin to imagine what passing a lifetime of eighty years might feel like; but here I am, in the twenty-first century, reflecting on my personal journey. I look back in amazement at the way that society has changed, particularly the role of women and the rapid development of technology, and wish to reflect on my own subjective experience of how these changes have affected me and how I have had to adapt to them. At the end of the writing process, I hope to have produced an entertaining account of my life that serves as a written amalgamation of the experiences and learning that has transformed me into the person I am in the present.

The ageing process has been kind to me. It is only recently that I have become aware of my chronological age as I have approached the big "Eight-Zero". Many years ago, I read a quote by Milton Shulman, a journalist who wrote a column in the Evening Standard, the London evening paper.

> *"Do not judge me on my chronological age but on my enthusiasm and productivity at this stage in my life."* – Milton Shulman

This seems very relevant for me. Despite my age, I feel that I still have something to contribute and so continue to work as a therapist. From the moment I wake in the morning, I look forward to what pleasures the day has in store for me. I lie there and think about the plans I have already made but also consider what surprises and untold treasures may be waiting to enchant me next. Change has always excited me and still does. I am still working to five-year plans and intend to do so until I pop my clogs. Obviously there are routines and rituals that have become an important feature of my day, such as going to the health club: me, for my aqua exercise, Henry, my husband, for swimming his allotted lengths of the pool.

There are a number of themes that feature throughout my story. The theme of "projects" recurs frequently. By this I mean that I have always needed something to look forward to and keep myself busy with. For this reason, I have been largely self-motivated for as long as I can remember. In fact, this attempt to write my memoirs can be viewed as another experiment in trying something new that challenges me, as writing has never been something that I have previously aspired to.

So what prompted me to begin this project? Well, every so often, I attend my "Stitched Up" group, which comprises of women whom I met whilst enrolled on a course called "Creative Textiles and Patchwork" at Burchett's Green Agricultural College. We set up the group on our own following the closure of the course and now meet on a regular basis at a local village hall. At one particular meeting, someone began a topic of conversation in which we discussed where we were and what we were doing when the Twin Towers collapsed. This was followed by where we were and what we were doing when John F Kennedy was assassinated, and so on. We all shared in telling our stories of how these historical events had impacted on our own lives. Later in the day, after returning home, I was provoked into undertaking a more rigorous reminiscence for the first time in ages, perhaps ever, concerning my life, my accomplishments and the people I have had the pleasure, in most cases, of meeting.

I have often been told that I should write down my story. It occurred to me that I should probably do this sooner than later as time is running out. Those who try to encourage me don't normally focus on such a fatalistic philosophy when they suggest the idea. It is more something I am conscious of. It is a fact: time is constantly running out for all of us. It is only when you reach a certain age that this universal truth becomes so intuitive.

As a 1930 vintage, I hope that I have attained some fascinating insights and maturity over the years. I am physically fit, sound of mind and very active. I am currently well and truly involved in the game of living and am still excited by projects undertaken or anticipated. I celebrated my seventieth birthday by inviting sixteen women, all of whom I felt had had a major influence on my life, for lunch. From then I have decided to count my birthdays as plus one, plus two, plus three etc. Whilst on a cruise to celebrate my eightieth birthday, I came to the decision that I would start on my next project and so I began writing my memoirs.

Another theme is the story of my evolution from a good girl to a good wife (*twice*) to, ultimately, a "WIT", Wise Woman in Training. It has been a search for both meaning and independence. I wasn't always aware of this or of the value of it; it is something that has become apparent to me during the last thirty years of my life. I didn't always recognise that what I was searching for was some kind of equality, the chance to be a person in my own right.

So, where to start?

I am an immigrant. These days, my status as an immigrant might classify me as a threat to some people living in the UK. The nature of what Britain has meant to the people who have been given shelter has changed for some over the years. In 1939, being allowed to enter the UK meant that my family and I could survive. There is no doubt in my mind that I wouldn't be writing this if our family hadn't been able to obtain a visa to enter the United Kingdom in 1939.

I love being an integrated citizen of this wonderful country. I have lived through eight decades of tremendous social change and have made every effort to adapt as much as possible. I like to think that it is my duty to fully embrace change, as it is the only constant in life.

The first ten years of my life were quite eventful, having been born into a Jewish family in Nazi Germany. I believe, quite fervently, that being part of a warm, loving family enabled me to take a lot of what happened on board without too much trouble, at least without causing any lasting damage. In the following seventy years or so, I have always felt that my life was a bonus. For this reason, my reactions to certain things might have been somewhat different to what would have been expected from me of other people, who had a more stable, grounded background.

The events described in this account will follow in chronological order, decade by decade. At the beginning of each chapter, I shall attempt to briefly summarise the relevant historical developments in order to put the events of my life in context. Some sort of contextual history will be placed at the beginning of each chapter, as well as being interspersed and interwoven within the text to add extra information or clarity when needed. Evaluating oneself within the context of a whole is important for telling any individual's life story. We are all touched in some way by the events that get remembered in history.

"No man is an island entire of itself… each man's death diminishes me, for I am involved in Mankind. Therefore send not to know for whom the bell tolls, it tolls for thee."- John Donne

CHAPTER ONE 1930-1939

The decade into which I was born was marked by economic and political turmoil. The world was plunged into hardship after the Wall Street Crash of 1929, beginning an era known as The Great Depression. The effects of this were felt across the Atlantic, triggering the rise of authoritarian regimes in many European countries, most notably the Third Reich in Germany. These events culminated in the beginning of the Second World War in 1939, with the Allies finally uniting against Hitler in response to German tanks and troops entering Polish borders. Many new technologies began to emerge during this time period, including long-distance aviation, radio, television and film.

MECONIUM ASPIRATION

I have been told on a number of occasions that I was late being born. A few years ago, I was speaking to a midwife, who explained to me the complications that can arise when a baby is born late, post forty weeks. She said that by prolonging its stay in its mother's womb, the unborn baby will begin to ingest amniotic fluid mixed with meconium. In other words, the baby will unknowingly begin to feed on its first stool. This condition is called meconium aspiration and causes pneumonia in new born babies. It can even result in still birth! I am not aware of the exact statistics or the rate of mortality connected to this terrible condition, but, whatever the odds were… still here!

KASSEL

Kassel, the German town in which I was born, is first acknowledged to have existed around 900 AD. Since then it has always been a provincial capital for the realms of North Hesse. Due to the Thirty Years' War, a large number of Huguenots immigrated to Kassel from France and brought with them their trade and skills. Over time Kassel became a city of considerable industrial and scientific significance, something which can be verified by taking a quick look around the Orangerie Museum, where all sorts of scientific equipment from the enlightenment period is on show. Kassel was already heavily industrialised before the Second World War, when it was then used for the mass-construction of trains, tanks and planes. Because of this, during the final years of the war, Kassel was duly targeted by English and American generals and was comprehensively bombed.

Kassel was once home to the Brothers Grimm, who wrote a lot of the fairy tales that we love and cherish today. With the helping hand of Walt Disney, the Brothers Grimm have been immortalised through the continued success of these wonderful stories, which include *Snow White and the Seven Dwarves*, *Cinderella* and *Sleeping Beauty*. Their residence has now been converted into a museum and houses a lot of interesting artefacts.

THE FAMILY

I was the youngest of five children. My eldest brother, Jack, was ten years older than me. When my mother became pregnant with me, he told her that he was ashamed of her, as she was thirty-three years old at the time. My mother had given birth to four children in five years. After Jack she gave birth to Paula, Herman and then Ruth. Four and a half years later I came along! I made my arrival on the 15 December, 1930. From the start I was the odd one out, as all of my brothers and sisters had been born during the 1920s.

It is strange how few meaningful conversations take place between parents and their children, especially my generation, whose parents had been born in the 1890s. I was close to my mother, and we talked about many things but never about her early experiences. I know virtually nothing about her youth.

My mother was born in Krakow, Poland, and had come to Germany at the age of eighteen. She was the eldest of five children, two brothers and two sisters. Her mother had been widowed when my mother was thirteen years old. Five years later, they all went to live in Leipzig.

Her mother came from an Orthodox Jewish family and wore what is known as a sheitel, which is a kind of wig that orthodox women wear once they get married. My mother didn't follow this tradition, neither did my two aunts.

She never spoke Polish, only German or Yiddish. When we came to England and started speaking English at home, initially she would only ever reply in German, however she soon picked up English as we would correct her or explain the meaning of an

English word we were using. This meant that we all became adept at switching between the two languages.

My mother was a very elegant woman and was highly intelligent. In fact, in later life I became aware that her intellect was far superior to that of my father. This was something I wasn't conscious of growing up, as my father was the dominant figure of the family, especially when it came to making decisions. He would almost always have the last word in any family dispute and often took the line of: "As I am the head of this household, you have to listen to me!" Of course, this wasn't particularly unusual for the times.

Every day, when he returned home from his office, he would turn off the radio, sit my mother down in front of him and, whilst he was having his cup of tea, regale her with a fastidious account of the events that had occurred during his day. He would then ask my mother's opinion, but, whenever she replied with anything contrary to his own opinion, he would shoot her down dogmatically, saying, "You don't understand!" I believe he just wanted her to approve of his actions, so as to vindicate his high opinion of himself, and, therefore, didn't respond well to her alternate views, which he took for criticism.

He was an excellent business man, incredibly skilled in accounts and entrepreneurial enterprises. Despite his authoritarian streak, he was also a devoted husband and loving father.

My father bore a broad, although largely unnoticeable, scar on his face, which he had acquired, no doubt painfully, as a two-year-old child. According to him, it was caused by an incident involving scalding water; an event that had also significantly affected his sense of smell.

During the winter my father would often take me with him to a café, in which he played cards with his friends. I would stand by his side, on my best behaviour, watching him play. My father's friends were all local business men like him, and, although the atmosphere during these games was often quite boisterous, I always felt comfortable there due to my father's presence. As the game progressed, the café would become swamped in cigar smoke, a smell which I have since always found pleasant. I was always willing to accompany my father on these outings and, regardless of the fact he was there to see his friends, I felt like it was a special time designated just for me and him. I guess I was always a little bit of a daddy's girl; although, my relationship with my mother was just as healthy.

I always felt that he was an extremely loving father. For instance, on these trips to the café he would always let me know how happy it made him to be walking with me and holding my hand. Sometimes, in the comfort of our home, I would enjoy combing his hair and shaping it in various styles. The others would laugh at me, but I didn't care.

I think it is so important for a child's development to be admired by the parent of the opposite sex. I have noticed that if children have the admiration of the parent of the opposite sex, they grow up feeling a greater sense of being lovable, are likely to have more confidence in dealing with the opposite sex and will be able to do so in a mature and appropriate manner.

MY FATHER'S SHOP

My father owned a men's outfitting business called *Kasseller Kleider Bourse*, which translates simply as Men's Outfitters of Kassel. It was situated on the corner of two streets, Muller Gasse and Ecke Pferdemarkt. We lived in two apartments above the shop that were linked together by a single corridor. The shop was a corner shop, which meant that our home was accessible both from an outside entrance into the building and an internal staircase from the shop premises. This meant that we had two front doors. I mention this as it takes on a greater significance later on in my story.

There was a large kitchen, living room, dining room, one bathroom and four bedrooms: one for my parents, one for my sisters, one for my brothers and another for our two housemaids, whose job it was to help my mother with her chores, as well as to look after me. As to where I slept, I believe it was with my sisters. I have one memory of Ruth arguing with my parents because they were forcing her to go to bed early, at my bedtime, because I was scared of the dark and needed someone to be in the room with me to sleep.

The only entertainment at home was the radio and gramophone in the living room. My mother was always singing excerpts from operas and, to this day, I love listening to light classical music on Classic FM. My father loved listening to the most famous tenor of the era, Enrico Caruso.

In photos of me from my early years, I am usually accompanied by one of our housemaids. This was because my mother was often busy helping my father in the shop and my brothers and sisters were at school. It fell upon the housemaids to look after me in the daytime. They would often take me on outings and daily excursions.

MY EARLIEST MEMORIES

As can be expected, my early memories are fairly vague. However, there were some highlights that remain with me to this day.

As in many continental towns there were rows of charming, little cafés by the river, to which my parents would take us for outings and ice creams on summer weekends. I loved sitting at the tables, which the café had set out along the banks of the river Fulda, devouring the delicious cakes that were on offer. We would watch the boats for hours and the people in them seamlessly drifting by. I remember thinking how happy everybody seemed to be out in the sunshine, so much so that you couldn't blame my younger self for thinking that the sun's rays were directly responsible for bringing happiness into the world. Sometimes my parents' friends would join us. I loved all the fuss they would make on my account.

I often went swimming with my brothers and sisters in the river. My eldest brother, Jack, had fixed a child seat at the rear of his bike, where I would sit, so that I wouldn't hold the others back on their way to the river. It was always a great treat to be taken to the river for a swim. I loved being in the water and became a competent swimmer from an early age. I realised quite quickly that, if I tried to swim underwater, I would always float back upwards. This gave me the confidence to swim without fear and, to this day, I still love swimming and try to do so daily.

When the weather was really hot, there was nothing as refreshing as jumping into the cool water. I loved swimming just beneath the water's surface and peering up at the sunlight as it tried to filter through the murky water, which always had a green and yellowish tint. I remember how the reeds and long grass kept moving to and fro with the current and being fascinated by the pebbles on the river bed. The river was full of minnows tirelessly darting around our feet. Sometimes I gathered a few pebbles and used them to play five-stones, a game of manual dexterity.

When I grew tired of playing about in the water, I would start to irritate my brothers and sisters by splashing them. Then I would sit on the blanket that was usually placed in the shade of a weeping willow tree, eating some of our picnic that we had brought with us. Our picnics consisted of sandwiches, cake, fruit and lovely homemade lemonade.

On one particular outing to the river it must have been exceptionally hot, and, even though there was plenty of shade from the surrounding trees and my brother had smothered me from head-to-toe in suntan lotion, I gradually started to burn. My siblings were occupied doing their own thing, playing their own games, and didn't notice that my complexion was taking on a rather rich shade of scarlet. I was aware that I was starting to cook but continued to jump in and out of the river. As I had picked some daisies, I was perfectly content playing on the rug making daisy chains for my wrists and hair.

When we arrived home, it became clear that I had developed all the classic symptoms of sunstroke. My poor brother received a stern telling off from my father, which seems unfair considering how he had given me so much pleasure that day by taking me down to the river. I think that my siblings must have seen me as a nuisance. They seemed to think that it wasn't fair that they were expected to have me tagging along with them on most of their outings. They just wanted to have fun, but had to constantly have an eye out for their little sister.

This incident didn't deter me in any way and I continued to be a sun worshipper for most of my adult life, as did the rest of my family. As soon as summer approached, we all took the opportunity to sit in the garden or go to a lido to swim. For my sisters and me, the aim was always to acquire a suntan. As both Paula and Ruth had black hair and brown eyes, as did the rest of my family, they had skin that was naturally darker and less likely to burn. I was the only one that had fair hair, blue eyes and pale skin. Unfortunately for me, my carefree attitude to the sun caught up with me. In 1998, I was diagnosed with a malignant melanoma on my shin; however, it was successfully removed without the need for any chemotherapy.

So from 1998 onward, sunbathing wasn't an option for me. The order of the day was sunblock, factor fifty, in order to avoid further damage. As I have always made a point of trying to see the positive side of things, I interpreted this as an opportunity to bid farewell to my fixation with sunbathing. Before, I would feel compelled, whenever the sun came out, to spend as much time as I could trying to get a suntan. But now, instead of wasting my summer days lounging around in the sun, I could do something far more productive. For instance, during the summer I would love nothing more than to sit in the shade on the Patio, listening to an Audio Book on my iPod and working on either a quilt or some tapestry looking at our beautiful garden that at that time of year looked groomed and lush and full of colour. I always experienced those times as peak moments. I was being read to, I was being creative, and in a delightful environment that had been created and tended by both Henry and me. This was absolute heaven on earth.

MEALTIMES

I used to love helping my mother cook. I was given many opportunities to do so as we had a lot of time to ourselves, while the others were attending school. She was a very good cook and encouraged me to help and learn from her. My mother baked beautiful cakes for my father's card evenings, when he invited all his friends from the café to our place. She also made delicious homemade donuts. I was a little bit tubby as a child because I enjoyed my food. On account of this, the family had a nickname for me: "Rollmops".

Fridays were always special, aside from the special Sabbath meal she prepared; my mother would bake two enormous trays of apple or plum tarts and various other yeast cakes. These were taken over to the bakery opposite our shop because they were of such a great size and quantity that our oven wasn't large enough. The cakes were for Saturday morning as my mother, being an orthodox Jew, didn't cook on the Sabbath. When Saturday morning came, we were allowed to go into the weekend dining room, where the baker's trays of cakes were placed on the sideboard, and, in a very continental manner, we just helped ourselves and drank our morning coffee.

During Passover, my mother worked extremely hard, changing the household over to have special crockery that was only used at this time of the year, when we only ate matzos and weren't allowed bread. She would prepare non-alcoholic grape wine for the children so that we could have our special "wine" for the wonderful Seder evening service. She was also a dab hand at making cherry brandy with Morella cherries, to which she added alcohol. After she had decanted it, she allowed us to have the cherries, which was another great treat.

We had a very large kitchen and all used to eat in there on weekdays. We always had our main meal at lunchtime. In the evening, my mother used to make sandwiches and various salads, such as tomato, cucumber or cabbage salad, to accompany the sandwiches. I know that, nowadays, many parents are concerned that their children don't eat enough, especially when it comes to eating their greens. I can assure you there was no such concern in our family. My mother never had to tell us to eat because, with five children to feed, as soon as the food was put on the table, we would all rush to fill our plates. A big platter of sandwiches was put on the table and, before anything was said, we all dived in and helped ourselves. Nothing was ever wasted. The girls who worked for us always joined in and were very much seen as a part of the family.

I had a habit of leaving my favourite sandwich for the end. One time Ruth asked me whether she could have a bite of my sandwich, and I grudgingly said, "No more than this", placing my finger as a marker just from the edge of the bread. She took a bite and, without realising it, bit quite hard into my finger. Naturally, I screamed. Ruth thought I was screaming because she had taken too much of my sandwich, but I was in real pain and was genuinely concerned that she had bitten off my entire finger. I learnt a big lesson that day: it doesn't pay to be stingy!

Ruth was a very generous person and, as a married woman later in life, she was the most wonderful hostess. The family would always meet up at her home in London, where she hosted the most fabulous dinner parties.

MY SIBLINGS

When it came to my brothers and sisters, Ruth was by far the closest to me. We were often inseparable. This was largely because she was closest to me in age, but also due to circumstance. My eldest brother Jack was much older than me and spent a large chunk of my early years studying at art school in Berlin, as did my sister Paula. Jack was a very good artist, and I still remember a portrait he painted of the Swedish actress, Greta Garbo, in the style of Picasso's muted Blue Period. I think the reason I remember this painting so vividly, and fondly, is because it was enormous. It spanned across the entirety of a wall in the store room of my father's shop. Paula studied dressmaking. These two were always together and more or less kept to themselves.

My brother Herman found himself stuck in the middle. Although he was two years older than Ruth, much closer in age than I was with her, his relationship with her was somewhat curtailed when he was sent off to Leipzig as a four-year-old. He returned to the family aged six, to commence school. However, during 1938, when there was the opportunity for him to go on a *Kinder transport* to stay with my Uncle Harry, he was once again sent away, this time to live with our uncle in Detroit in the years immediately prior to the war. I now know that he found this incredibly hard to deal with. Even though his trip to Detroit was a blessing in disguise, as it spared him the horrors of Nazi anti-Semitism, he couldn't understand why he had to leave his family for a second time. It wasn't acknowledged then, as much as it is now, that parents' decisions can inadvertently affect their children in so many different ways, even if these decisions were made with nothing but the best of intentions.

With the rest of the siblings either busy or in absentia, it became Ruth's role in the family to look after me when my parents were occupied and the nursemaids weren't around. She had been the youngest for four years prior to my birth. Now that my role was to be the youngest, she took to her new role as my mentor/ babysitter with enthusiasm, and our relationship blossomed; although, I imagine that looking after a baby was often a burden and that she often came to regret being stuck with a sister that was four years her junior.

Ruth would often get into trouble on my account. Ruth was a tomboy and thus fearless, whereas I was far less adventurous. One day there was an incident when Ruth and I were out for a walk. She ran down a steep slope and then dared me to follow. There was a patch of gravel at the bottom, upon which I fell and made a mess of my knees. Poor Ruth got into trouble; I still have the scar on my right knee today.

A TOUCH OF HOLLYWOOD

One day, my nursemaid took me to the cinema for a treat. I don't remember the reason for this indulgence but do remember the star of the movie, the famous child star of the Thirties, Shirley Temple.

I was absolutely enthralled with what I saw; however, my attention was directed exclusively at this beautiful little girl, who was about the same age as me at that time. I was charmed by her personality, which seemed to shine so brightly through the screen that it got under my skin and right to the heart of my youthful sensibility. Even though Hollywood seemed so far away, almost like it was on a completely different planet, during those glorious moments when she was up on that screen, I felt like I had found a great friend. Nevertheless, I was really quite jealous of her wonderful mop of golden curls, and her dimples made me feel as if my face was missing something. I can recall pushing my fingers into my cheeks in an attempt to simulate the same "look".

If you were to ask me to tell you what happened in the film, I couldn't. My mind is blank on that one. I have no recollection of the plot but can fondly recall the melody and lyrics of the film's hit song, "On the good ship lollipop". I remember dancing around the apartment singing the chorus over and over, as I wanted to be a movie star just like Shirley Temple. I recall standing in front of my mother's dressing mirror convinced that, by singing and dancing in front of it, I would somehow magically be teleported onto the big screen. The joy that this song brought to Little Margot is something which has always stuck with me.

Looking back on those days, I am delighted that I was fortunate enough to have the opportunity to live out my early childhood in such a safe environment and with such lovely family experiences, whilst all around me the adults were beginning to acknowledge the dangers that were soon to be thrust upon them, dangers that would soon drive the whole world towards chaos and such unthinkable horror.

RITA

My very best friend was a girl called Rita, who was so pretty and always wore a big ribbon in her hair. Rita lived only a few turnings away, so we used to play together regularly either at her house or mine. Looking back, we probably spent more time at mine, because, at Rita's place, her mother would make us take off our shoes and generally maintained a far stricter code of conduct than I was used to. With a family containing five lively children, our house wasn't kept to the same standard of tidiness, despite two live-in maids.

Writing this now makes me feel sad, as Rita perished in a concentration camp with both her parents. I didn't find this out until quite recently, in 2000.

From about the age of five, we were given a great deal of freedom to walk around and explore our local neighbourhood. We were sufficiently warned, as children are today, not to take sweets from or walk off with strange men. One day, whilst we were out playing, a man approached us and asked us whether we would like some sweeties. We both said no and quickly ran back to one of our houses. Even then, people were well aware that there were deviants around, but the situation was handled in a way that made children aware of the danger in a sensible way without panicking them.

ANNA'S FARM

One year, my nursemaid, Anna, took me to her family farm during the Easter Holiday. I had never seen a farm before and was struck immediately by the strong smell of hay from the barnyard. It was a smell that was completely new to me. There was so much for me to absorb in this exciting environment, including the massive horses that were used for so many different tasks on a farm in those days. Anna's family also kept cows, which enabled me to drink fresh milk in the morning. I was delighted to learn that this fresh milk was so much more flavoursome than the milk I was used to drinking. I was also allowed to feed the brown and white chickens running around the yard. During the Easter weekend, Anna boiled some eggs, painted them and then hid them in various places around the farm for me to find. It was so much fun to run around searching for these lovely objects.

Before going to the farm, I had never ridden a horse. Anna put me on this enormous carthorse that was hugely intimidating, yet, at the same time, strangely exciting. There was a time in my early twenties when I thought that riding might be a good way for me to exercise, so I tried it again. There were stables connected to Hyde Park, and I thought it might be interesting to go riding in Rotten Row, which was quite fashionable at the time and not too far from where I lived in Bayswater, opposite Kensington Gardens. Whenever I got back on a horse, I remembered that Easter holiday and the fun that I had. However, I was never truly comfortable riding and remained almost childishly fearful of falling off, so quickly gave up.

Many years later, in 2000, I was invited back to Kassel by the *Oberburgermeister* (the mayor) for a reunion, which had been arranged for all the Jewish Burghers who were forced to leave Germany during the 1930s. We had our photos taken by a journalist who accompanied the group. Anna saw the pictures in the newspaper, recognised the photo of myself and her and made inquiries via her granddaughter. Following my return to the UK, we entered into a brief correspondence, but, unfortunately, her mind was going. We never got the chance to meet up again.

Over the years we had a number of housemaids, all of whom spent large periods of time looking after me. Anna is the one who stands out in my memory the most. I am not sure whether this is because of our recent correspondence or simply because I genuinely shared more memorable moments with her than any of the others.

One day, when Anna was taking me out on my daily walk, we came across a reasonably large crowd gathering at the side of the road. In front of me passed an open-top car containing a rotund individual decorated in the most ostentatious army uniform with medals covering every inch of his jacket. I think I must have asked Anna who the "Big, fat man" was. She told me it was Hermann Goering. I later verified the truth of this memory, as Goering had, in fact, travelled to Kassel on that date to visit the armaments factory.

SCHOOL

During my first few years, I spent a lot of time playing by myself and was comfortable doing so. Every morning I would watch my brothers and sisters heading off to school. I think that being left to one's own devices makes children become creative as they have to come up with clever ways to amuse themselves. I adored dressing up, as most little girls do. My mother, who was an incredibly elegant woman, never objected to me playing with her cosmetics and trying on her shoes, scarves and jewellery. I dressed my dolls, skipped and played ball and, of course, had my little girlfriend, Rita, who lived around the corner. The years flew by until I went to Kindergarten aged about four.

School did not start till age six. I cannot remember whether I was able to read prior to starting school, but I know that after one year in education I was able to read and write, do arithmetic and could also read and write in Hebrew. It was most fortuitous that I acquired the fundamental skills early, because in 1938, following *Kristallnacht*, all the Jewish schools in Germany closed. This meant that I only attended school in Germany for about eighteen months.

I have attached a photo of me on my first day at school. On this special day, all the children were given a large cone filled with fruit and sweets as a celebration of the beginning of their education. The teachers were very strict in Germany and armed themselves with canes to let you know if you were misbehaving. This was never a problem for me as I was always the model student. Even from a very young age, I loved learning. As I grew older, this urge to improve myself through education never left me and even grew stronger.

I feel that my early childhood made me feel very loved and secure. I think that it enabled me to cope with many adverse situations later in life and helped me to understand the importance of secure attachment and the effect this has on all relationships.

KRISTALLNACHT

By 1936, the atmosphere had begun to change. I understand now how much of a difficult task it would have been for my parents to explain to me the complex nature of Nazi beliefs and Hitler's determination to rally against the Jews. All I was told was that there were certain people who didn't like Jewish people and that I had to be particularly careful and well-behaved around anyone in uniform, regardless of whether they were soldiers or policemen. Whenever one of the nursemaids took me out for a walk, we would always retreat into a shop or doorway if we came across any troops marching by. They were well aware that the officials might question why a little girl with blond hair, blue eyes and no apparent Semitic features wasn't joining in with the Hitler salute.

Certain restrictions were put in place to distance the Jewish population from the rest of Germany. If you had been born into the Jewish faith, you were now considered stateless. In fact, following *Kristallnacht*, identity papers were stamped with a large "J" for Jude, and all first names were prefixed with Sarah for women and Israel for men.

On the evening of 9 November, 1938, the Nazi regime encouraged and authorized brutal riots aimed at controlling the Jewish community in Germany. The Night of Broken Glass, *Kristallnacht*, saw Jewish homes, shops, synagogues, community centres, schools, hospitals and cemeteries pillaged, looted and destroyed, all in the name of a ruthless, yet completely official, Nazi anti-Semitism. It is recorded that 267 synagogues were destroyed, 7,500 Jewish businesses ransacked and at least 91 Jewish people killed.

As previously mentioned, my father owned a menswear store, *Kasseller Kleider Bourse*, a double fronted shop on the corner of two streets. The last time I saw it was in 2000. It has now become a Thai restaurant.

Before visiting in 1998, I hadn't returned to Kassel. The sad reason for this was that I felt I wouldn't be able to trust anyone older than I, as they would have been adults during the war years and would have played some part in the atrocities. I couldn't help but feel like this despite the fact that, when it mattered most, our neighbours had been incredibly supportive to us during our troubles. I don't know if this was right or wrong of me; it is just how I felt.

Why is it that children drift through life never asking their parents meaningful questions about their life experiences? I never had a serious conversation with my parents about how they perceived the events of *Kristallnacht*. I am sure they would have had a far more complete picture of what had really happened than the one I am left with. Unfortunately, as I left it too late, I can only draw a picture of that event through the eyes of a seven-year-old.

I have no idea of the time of day, except that it was dark outside. We were hiding in the room above the shop, which was a very large lounge/dining room that our family used for special occasions. I can only assume that my parents gathered us in this room because it had windows looking out onto both streets, allowing them to see everything that was happening. I am not sure whether my parents received any warning of what was going to happen, or if it was all a complete shock for them. Like I said, this was never discussed by the family.

Jack and Paula weren't present as they were both studying at art school in Berlin. Herman had left a few months earlier on a *Kinder transport* (Children's Transport) to live with Uncle Harry, my father's brother, who had immigrated to Detroit during the 1920s. *Kinder transport* was the name given to the rescue efforts that took Jewish children away from the dangers in Germany and brought them to Britain and America between 1938 and 1940. I recall my mother, father, Ruth and grandfather being there on that evening.

There was a lot of shouting in the streets, as the riots grew progressively violent. I sat close to my mother away from the windows, unable to see much of anything through the darkness. It felt like whatever was happening out there was getting closer and closer, encroaching upon our home, which had now taken on the role of our hiding place. First, we were struck by the sound of shattering glass, as the crowd broke the plate-glass windows of my father's shop front. This was followed by a loud crash as a brick smashed right through the window of our front room. My mother screamed. Fortunately, we had net curtains, so no one was cut by flying glass; but now there was light shining into the room, as there was a street light on the corner. Soon after the brick broke through the glass window, we heard people entering the shop directly beneath us.

We were unbelievably lucky as some people shouted that the Adler's, my maiden name, didn't actually live above the shop. This was probably the best thing that could have happened to us. Really, it was the thing that saved us. If our living quarters had been on the ground floor, who knows what might have happened. There was a lot of noise downstairs, but no one came up to where we were hiding. Nevertheless, the shop windows were all smashed, the shop was looted and all the merchandise stolen. We could hear all this as it took place just below where we were standing. For all the raucous noise and terror that came with it, not one person came up the internal stairway from the storage room and into our home, and the riots eventually died down. We were safe, for the time being.

I was far too young to comprehend what was going on, but I was petrified. How was a child supposed to react to something like that? In all honesty, I was unable to comprehend the full significance of what was going on. I was simply struck by the innate and instinctively visceral nature of terror, which was incited just as much by the fear in the faces of my family as it was by the loud noises of the crowd outside.

My paternal grandfather must have been more frightened than anyone else. He knew, first hand, the potential horror of such fervent anti-Semitism. He was born and spent his youth in Poland and had witnessed all kinds of anti-Semitic feelings there, often leading to Pogroms and other random killings. That was one of the reasons he came to live in Germany at the turn of the twentieth century. He must have been about seventy years old on *Kristallnacht*. He was an orthodox Jew, with a long beard. I remember often sitting on his lap and looking beneath his beard to see whether he wore a tie like my father.

THE AFTERMATH

In the morning, the Gestapo marched into our home and took my father away to Buchenwald concentration camp.

Of course, we had no idea where they were taking him or whether we would see him again. There was no explanation from the Gestapo; they just took him away. The idea of concentration camps and death camps were completely unknown to most people at the time. It took years, even decades after 1945, to fully comprehend what had happened in these hellish places. In 1938, the words "concentration camp" had no real meaning for us at all.

As hard as I try to recall my father's abduction, my mind draws blank. Since working as a counsellor debriefing victims of posttraumatic stress, I can offer an informed explanation for this. When something happens to you that is so vastly different from anything you have previously experienced, your cognitive functions can fail to comprehend what is happening to you. I have worked with many clients who suffer from this same inability to recall difficult memories. The memory might be there, it is just that the event was beyond comprehension at the time. It shouldn't be seen as a failure of memory, but more a failure of the initial ability to comprehend the original experience at the time.

After my father was taken, my mother was made to sweep up all the glass and debris from the broken shop windows and then to board up all the windows.

Following *Kristallnacht*, my parents, who had already applied for a visa to the United States in 1936, realised that this wouldn't be granted in time. My mother contacted her sister Fanny, who lived in Paris. Her husband was a very successful international fur trader, who specialised in broadtail and mink furs and visited London regularly to attend the Hudson Bay Auctions, where furs were traded on an international scope. He contacted the British Consulate to inform them of the gravity of the situation and was granted Exit Visas for my parents and for all four of us children. Our solicitor was then able to provide the evidence of this to the Gestapo, and we were given permission to leave; however, this permission was conditional and allowed us a three-month window to move away, starting from 12 December, 1938, to 12 March, 1939. We arrived in London on the 8 March, 1939. It was quite a close call!

I have been eternally grateful to this uncle because, without a doubt, I wouldn't be here today if he had been unable to obtain that visa. Sadly, we learnt sometime after the war that our solicitor, his wife and daughter all died in Auschwitz.

In the months before we could get away, we had to live under Nazi restrictions. Jews weren't allowed to go into ordinary food stores, but had one store in town that would now provide food for the entire Jewish population of Kassel. We had maintained our good relationship with most of our neighbours. They helped us out at great risk to themselves by secretly smuggling various provisions to us. For instance, the dairy shop next-door provided us with dairy products each morning.

The Jewish schools were all closed. Anyone working for a Jewish family was told that it was illegal and demeaning to work for Jews. Our lovely maids, who had become such an integral part of our family, had to leave.

Once we had received our documents, both the visa from the British Consulate and the permit to leave Germany, we began to pack up our belongings to despatch them to England. We were aware that, prior to leaving our premises, our things would be thoroughly searched and examined and that anything of value would be confiscated.

It was a safety precaution to make all children aware of whatever actions their parents were thinking of taking. This was so they wouldn't accidentally betray their parents at the most inconvenient of moments. My mother had a few pieces of valuable jewellery. As we were leaving with virtually nothing else of any value, she and my father decided to hide these items in a large enamelled container, labelled *Salz* (Salt), on the wall of the kitchen near the cooker. When the Gestapo came into our home with their big helmets and jackboots, they turned over the sofas and chairs and opened and inspected all the cupboards, looking for anything of value. Ruth and I were sitting in the kitchen whilst all this was going on. I was terrified by these men with their black uniforms and large, metal helmets. To me they looked like giants. A likeness to Darth Vader now comes to mind.

I was conscious of wanting to divert my eyes anywhere but directly at them and their investigation. Knowing where our valuables were hidden, I was also conscious not to look in that direction. I tried desperately hard not to look up at the kitchen wall and, feeling very frightened, just sat quietly, keeping my head down and holding Ruth's hand. I didn't dare look at her, as I didn't want to see her fear. I was used to her always looking after me and being so brave and strong. I didn't want to change this perception of her, especially not at that moment, as I don't know how I would have reacted if I had looked into her eyes and saw that she was as terrified as I was. Eventually, the gestapo left without finding a thing, but had created such unnecessary chaos. Once again, my poor parents had to clear up. We all pitched in to get this done.

As I am writing this I am reflecting on my parents' bravery, or is it more apt to describe it as foolishness, that they could risk so much for a little financial security. This was even more of a concern considering that my father had only recently been allowed back from Buchenwald due to the efforts of our solicitor, who had made a petition to the authorities saying that my father was needed to wind up his business.

My father had spent six weeks in Buchenwald. He never spoke of his experience.

LEAVING KASSEL

In March 1939, the move away from Kassel started. Some of our belongings had been packed. Those that the Germans had allowed us to take with us were sent to London via shipping line. We were only allowed to carry with us a small amount of our clothing. The family spent the next few days at my uncle's house, which was just across the road from ours. My recollection of this time is imprecise, but, on reflection, this period in my memory is accompanied by a general sense of doom and gloom, perhaps because it was taking place in the short dark days of February and March, but more likely because everyone was downcast and subdued by the terrible fear that something bad would happen to us before we could escape.

We were travelling to England from the Hook of Holland, so took a train from Kassel to the ferry. The train stopped at the border between Holland and Germany, where German soldiers came aboard and searched every carriage in case anyone was taking anything with them that wasn't permitted. My parents were aware that the carriages would be searched by the SS and so, prior to boarding the train, had given both my sister and myself a small tin box, containing, guess what!, the jewels that had previously been hidden from the Gestapo in the salt container.

At the border, when the German guards came on board to check the documents, my parents sent us into the corridor, and we remained there until we had crossed the border into Holland. Obviously, in retrospect, this was a risky choice, but in difficult times people are forced to make decisions that aren't always wise. I was quite early in life to become a smuggler.

I have been told that our crossing was one of the choppiest across the Channel for a long time. So much so that virtually everyone on board was seasick, including me. Eventually, we arrived in Harwich and moved on straight to London.

I can't help but feel that my family was most fortunate, considering what happened to the Jewish families who didn't get out of Hitler's Germany in time. Why were we so lucky, when others weren't? It has made it hard for me not to believe in some kind of fate.

CHAPTER TWO 1939-1949

The first half of the decade was occupied by the Second World War, although the consequences were felt for decades to come. The conflict began in Continental Europe, although it eventually spread all over the globe, with The United States joining the Allies' cause in response to the Japanese bombing of Pearl Harbour. After the war, a number of new institutions, such as the United Nations, the Welfare State and the Bretton Woods institutions were set up to provide stability and security across the globe, so that a war of such magnitude would never be repeated. Around the same time, many states sought independence such as India, Pakistan and Israel etc. With the war came a surge in technological development, including computers and nuclear power.

A CASE OF DIPTHERIA

On arriving in the UK, my family was allocated accommodation in the East End of London at the Mansell Street Shelter, a refuge for Jewish immigrants arriving from various parts of Europe. It was a short-term solution until my parents found a flat for us to live in. East London was suggested as a good place to look, as there was a large Jewish community there, and Yiddish was spoken. As my parents didn't speak any English and neither did any of the children, it made a lot of sense. All I can really recall of these temporary living arrangements were the communal accommodation on camp beds.

As soon as we arrived into London, it was obvious that I was unwell. My mother was adamant that I had tonsillitis, as I kept complaining of a sore throat. Due to the large number of people living in the shelter, with more constantly arriving, there were many doctors around. It didn't take long for me to be seen to. I was diagnosed with diphtheria and transferred to an isolation unit in a nearby hospital. My mother was obviously distressed at this and insisted upon the inaccuracy of the diagnosis. In spite of my mother's persistence, I soon found myself in an ambulance on the way to the hospital and away from my family.

On arrival, I was immediately examined, given some sort of injection and then transferred to the ward in which I would spend the next month. Thinking about it now, the ward looked exactly like the set of *Carry on Doctor*. Everything was unusually bright and exceptionally shiny.

The matron made her rounds every morning and would check that our sheets were tucked in properly and that the children had been washed all over. The nurses, in their caps and starched uniforms, looked very smart. I imagine the hospital staff must have communicated to me in German, as I knew no English at all. They were all very kind to me. One of the nurses gave me a German/English dictionary and I think that this, along with being immersed in an exclusively English speaking environment, played a large part in speeding up my learning.

Did I miss my parents or siblings? I must have done at first, but I cannot remember. The kindness and warmth of the hospital staff made it surprisingly easy to adapt to this strange environment, which would have been highly distressing for any eight-year-old girl, let alone one who found herself alone in a completely foreign land.

After four weeks I was released from quarantine. In those days, on entering a hospital as a patient, your clothes were taken away and probably burnt. I can only speculate about this, because I never saw my clothes again! They kept a ragtag supply of mixed clothing for the patients to wear as their health improved. When my mother first saw me, she remarked that I looked like an orphan. I was dressed in black stockings and a dress that didn't quite fit. My mother was always very proud of how she dressed her daughters. I am sure she couldn't wait to get me home and into more elegant clothing. For instance, when we were young, my sister Ruth and I wore matching dresses for high days and holidays. A dressmaker would come to our home and make identical dresses for us.

SIDNEY STREET

On my return to the family, I found that they had moved into a new building on Sidney Street, a three-bedroom apartment with a bathroom, balcony and a decent-sized kitchen. My parents had one bedroom, Jack another and Paula, Ruth and I shared the third. Our flat was on the second floor.

The apartment below us was occupied by a kind, friendly family. What I didn't realise until many years later was that the couple and their young children were related to my current husband, Henry. The woman was his father's sister, his Aunt Rosy, and the children, who were about the same age as he was, were evidently his cousins. Their family were very kind to us. For instance, when Ruth and I returned from our first stint away on evacuation, their father drove my mother to pick us up in his car.

The flats were on three floors with a balcony overlooking the courtyard, which was mostly used as a play area by the children. There was some personal storage space for the tenants; however, when all of our furniture and other belongings finally arrived from the docks, the container was too big for our allotted space and had to be kept outside in the courtyard. This large, mysterious container captured the imagination of the children, whose intrigue fuelled many games of guessing what strange and magical goodies were inside. They would have been disappointed by the banal reality of its actual contents, which were mainly just old sheets, dirty cushions and broken parts of furniture that had fallen apart in transit.

The building was called Sandhurst House, as the entrance turned out onto Sandhurst Street; although many of the apartments faced out onto Sidney Street, a turning off Whitechapel Road close to the London Hospital and the Courage Brewery. When out and about playing with my friends, I often saw the enormous cart horses pulling the drays that carried the barrels of beer. I felt really sorry for the horses in icy weather, as they frequently had difficulty getting a grip on the cobbles.

At the time, Sidney Street was infamous for an incident that had occurred there in 1911. The siege of Sidney Street was a gruelling gunfight between two local gangs that resulted in two fatalities. It made the headlines not only for the violence but because of the supposed involvement of the then Home Secretary, Winston Churchill.

When the summer school term commenced, I was enrolled at a local infants school in the senior class, as it was decided that this would be the best way for me to catch up with reading English. The idea was that in September, when the new school year dawned, I would have learnt enough that I could start the junior school and be able to make sense of the different subjects. One of the teachers gave me the book *Heidi* as a present. I cherished this gift and read it several times from cover to cover.

In the end I never went to the junior school, as war was declared against Germany. Ruth and I, along with all the young children that lived in major cities, were evacuated to the countryside.

EVACUATION

Official evacuation was declared on 31 August and began, in earnest, on 1 September, two days before the declaration of war.

Equipped with our gas masks and name tags, Ruth and I were bundled onto a train to evacuate the city. The train journey was surprisingly brief, our final destination being Staines. We were paraded through the streets by our teachers, who would knock on every door to see whether we would be welcomed. Strict instructions had been given to ensure that Ruth and I weren't separated. We came as a package, all or nothing. This prolonged our parade, as a suitable household willing to take both of us proved hard to find. Luckily it wasn't raining. I actually remember it being a particularly sunny day. Eventually a pleasant woman, Mrs Wood, invited us into her home.

It was an altogether alien experience for us being thrown into this very traditional English environment. Since moving from Germany, our family had kept up its continental European and Jewish customs. Now, Ruth and I found ourselves immersed in, what I can only describe as, a definitively English household. Our arrival must have been as difficult for Mrs Wood as it was for us. She had borne two sons, who had now grown up and were away fighting in the army. My guess is that she wasn't used to having two little girls in her home, especially two little foreign girls. Although she tried her best to accommodate us as well as she could, it was obvious that we were a strain on her. This created a little tension, especially at meal times.

The food Mrs Wood served to us was very different to what we were used to. Our palate was accustomed to a continental, kosher style of cooking. This kind old woman couldn't understand why a little eight-year-old girl was rejecting her best cooking, such as rabbit, parsnips and pork pies. Ruth, who was thirteen by that time, was a little more diplomatic and managed to eat most of the food offered. I frequently left most of my dinner to the constant dismay of Mrs Wood.

In spite of my refusal to eat her dinners, Mrs Wood was always kind to me. As a matter of fact, she went out of her way to knit a series of woollen vests for me. Although she had the best intentions, it soon became apparent that I was allergic to the wool, as I couldn't stop scratching myself. I had never worn that type of garment in my life. My mother had always dressed me in cotton vests. I was incredibly grateful for this kind gesture, but unable to wear the vests.

Evacuation posed a series of difficult problems for everybody, both practical and emotional. The personal anxieties suffered by the children, who had to leave their homes and families, unsure whether they would see their parents again, were huge. Education was one practical problem facing these rural communities. Because of the huge influx of children, all needing to be placed in school, children were only allowed to have lessons for half a day. Ruth and I were obviously lovable, well-behaved girls, because one of the teachers wanted to adopt us. I have no idea what my mother made of that.

Whilst we were living with Mrs Wood, we were permitted to go to the local cinema. Ruth managed to get me into films that, on reflection, were completely inappropriate for a child of my age. She was obsessed with horror movies. To this day, I can recall the titles of two films that gave me nightmares and put me off the genre forever. The first film was *Bride of Frankenstein*, the second, *The Return of the Zombies*. Just by looking at the names of these films, you could tell that they weren't appropriate for a child of my age, but in those days children of any age could walk into an auditorium and watch whatever they pleased. I remember resting my head in Ruth's lap to cover my eyes. Oh, the joys of childhood and having older siblings!

INTERNMENT

Ruth and I returned to London in June 1940. My mother had decided she was missing us too much and felt it was safe for us to return. London hadn't been hit as hard by German bombing as was first expected. We were very pleased to return home; although, when we returned, we found that our father had once again found himself in a troublesome situation.

One of the most controversial issues in England during the Second World War was the internment of "enemy aliens" on the Isle of Man in May 1940. That many of these people were Jewish refugees and, therefore, hardly likely to be sympathetic to the Nazi regime was a complication no one bothered to try and unravel. The government of the time were unable to differentiate between genuine refugees escaping from persecution and potential spies for the Third Reich. As a precaution, everybody who had emigrated out of Nazi Germany had to be treated as German and Austrian nationals. In one Isle of Man camp over eighty per cent of the internees were Jewish refugees.

When we returned our father wasn't at home. He had been interned. I can only imagine his feelings when, once again, he was confined in a camp. This time by a nation that had offered him freedom and shelter. Fortunately, an outcry in parliament led to the first releases in August of the same year, and he returned to us just before the onset of the London Blitz.

PAULA'S BOYFRIEND

During our evacuation, Paula had met a very nice young man called Orky. She was seventeen at the time, and he was about twenty. He was a local boy and had recently joined the army. I recall the name of his regiment, the Sherwood Foresters.

Orky was a tall, handsome young man with striking blond hair. He was also very kind and, whenever he came over, would play games with me and sometimes even bring me sweets. One day, he brought me a beautiful, little doll. I was absolutely thrilled to receive it as, like most children in those days, I didn't have many toys.

Paula and he were very much in love.

Eventually, he was called to duty and stationed in the Far East. Not long after, we heard he had died in action. Naturally, Paula was devastated. What nobody realised was the effect this loss had on me. I did something that I didn't understand until fifty years later, when I took part in a training weekend for bereavement counselling. I smashed the beautiful doll against a wall and broke it. The family were furious with me, but I couldn't explain to them how hurt and upset I was. I think in those days people weren't aware that death affects all members of the family, not just the adults. Children were often excluded from funerals in the early twentieth century. It was often the case that, when they grew up, they would regret their parents' decision not to let them say a final farewell to their parent, siblings or grandparents.

THE LONDON BLITZ

Between 7 September, 1940, and 10 May, 1941, German air fighters carried out sustained bombing of Britain and Northern Ireland. These tactics used by Germany were referred to as *Blitzkrieg* (lightening) due to the speed and relentlessness of the attacks. London was bombed for seventy-six consecutive nights along with many other cities deemed strategically important across the country. More than one million houses were affected by the bombing just in London and forty thousand civilians were killed nationwide.

It all began quite suddenly. We saw the sky light up a bright orange as the German bombers launched wave upon wave of attacks on the London dockland. I remember standing outside our apartment, looking up at the sky and being bowled away by what looked like the most beautiful sunset I had ever and would ever see. An ominous shade of rouge hung in the sky, terrifyingly vibrant. If it wasn't for people screaming, "The docks are burning!" I would have genuinely thought it was just an exquisite sunset and would have sat there quietly admiring it. Instead, we were all thrown into a sudden state of panic, as no one had been expecting such a brutal attack.

My brother Jack was an air raid warden and would tell us gruesome stories in the morning, when he returned home after a long night rescuing people from the wreckage. Our apartment building was surrounded by rows and rows of small houses. His job was to scour through those that had been hit, searching for injured people and doing whatever he could to help them. He was only eighteen at the time, and his evenings would be spent dragging dead bodies from the ruins. His accounts of the devastation were like something out of a horror movie. I don't know how but he quickly became acclimatised to this extreme level of carnage and gore.

During the daytime, my friends and I used to search for pieces of shrapnel amongst the rubble of houses that had been damaged during the night. We would play amongst the debris as if it were our own makeshift playground. We were perhaps too young to fully understand the implications of the damage, that these bits of rubble used to be part of people's homes and were the physical manifestation of a lifetime of memories lost. Now it belonged to no one; it was just detritus lying in the street, scattered all around us.

On a bright day, we could see fighter planes passing overhead above the silver-coloured barrage balloons. But as evening approached, anxiety returned. All the inhabitants of our building gathered in one of the ground floor apartments, which had been reinforced with steel. The bombing continued night after night.

For a while our block of flats escaped unharmed; however, one night in 1941, we received a direct hit. Our building was crashed into by a parachute-retarded modified marine mine, the largest air-dropped ordinance in use by the Luftwaffe at that time, weighing about 500KG. These would drop towards their target at 40mph and were fitted with a parachute system, because if they reached a greater speed the bomb would disintegrate before landing.

The reinforced shelter on the ground floor saved all of our lives. After the initial panic, someone took charge and we were ordered to move out onto the street. Someone directed us toward an emergency exit and helped us clamber out. Paula went out first, followed by Ruth and then me. As all of this happened, my parents were separated from us. When we realised that they weren't there, Paula quickly took on the responsibility of our safety, as you would expect from the eldest. She ushered us toward a nearby brick-built shelter, and we ran as fast as we could.

From March 1940, many public shelters were installed in appropriate locations due to the surprise nature of the German attacks. These communal shelters were usually made up of 14-inch brick walls and 1-foot thick reinforced concrete roofs and could hold around fifty people. The government provided the materials for these to be built as quickly as possible, but materials soon ran out due to excessive demand as attacks became more frequent and ferocious. The public was alarmed by the poor performance of the early street shelters and this had a negative effect on public confidence. Their walls would crumble under the strain and impact of any nearby blast, causing the concrete roof to fall onto the helpless occupants.

We forced our way into the shelter alongside a swarm of other people. There was constant panic and screaming as bombs continued to fall. When we finally felt we were safe, a bomb fell just outside the shelter, shaking the structure to what must have been close to its breaking point. Happily, it didn't collapse. No one inside was hurt, but the shelter was engulfed in a wave of thick dust, which we all started choking on. I cannot recall what happened next, but…

…Still here.

CROUCH END

Following the destruction of Sandhurst House, we were fortunate enough to find a Victorian house in the Crouch End area of London. This came about because Jack was romantically involved with a lovely girl called Jessie Weinberg. Her family had also been living in our apartment block before its destruction. Even though there was an extreme housing shortage in London due to the destruction caused by the constant bombing, Mrs Weinberg had found a large house and had offered to share it with our family.

I had never lived in a house with a garden or in a building where our home was two stories high. In the garden we had a Nissan Shelter, a corrugated structure which was banked up with earth.

Our family's life centred round the kitchen/living room more than anywhere else in the house. Our converted kitchen had a fireplace, a gas stove and a dining table, which was later replaced by a Morrison Shelter. The Morrison Shelter was an ugly cage-like structure consisting of a solid 3mm steel plate on top and set of wire meshes down the sides. Should there be an air raid the residents were advised to get underneath this table as a protection in case the house collapsed. It didn't matter that it looked out of place in the kitchen; it was one of many necessary precautions needed to ensure the family's safety.

The sash window of the kitchen was taped across with masking tape to prevent glass from flying everywhere as a result of a blast from an explosion. There was also a small sofa, assorted chairs and a radio in this room. We were often visited by mice that would periodically scamper across the room as we sat around the fire. I liked to think the mice enjoyed sharing our home with us, even if we weren't so keen on them. Somehow they always seemed to avoid the mouse traps that had been strategically placed.

Due to a fuel shortage heating became a luxury, and so the house was bitterly cold. On winter mornings my father would get up and light the fire so that we wouldn't have to wake to near-arctic conditions. We would all sit in front of the fire for hours, which left a peculiar pattern on the front of our legs where the heat had started to burn them a little. Every morning I would bring my school clothes in and dress in front of the fire. Perhaps the worst part of all was that the bathroom was so cold and the water was close to freezing. Washing became an almighty trial, and I generally rushed through my morning routine to get back to my place in front of the fire. My mother usually inspected whether my neck had been washed and would promptly send me straight back to the bathroom demanding that I wash properly.

The bathroom was on the first floor and was used by everyone in the house. Baths were strictly limited to once a week and to only five inches of hot water. This was all part and parcel of keeping to the restrictions set on account of the fuel shortage. It was a time of real caution and cutbacks; for instance, we would use old newspaper cut into neat squares more often than not that was my job, as the only alternative to toilet paper.

For breakfast we made good use of a couple of toasting forks. We would prepare toast by piercing the bread and holding it up to the fire. My father made sandwiches for everyone to take to work. My school provided me with dinner, and, in those days, we also were given a small bottle of milk at break time. At one stage, I was allotted the role of milk monitor. My job was to ensure everyone received their milk and that none of it was wasted; a responsibility I took seriously.

Paula, Ruth and I shared a bedroom with one double bed and a single. As the eldest Paula took the single bed, leaving me and Ruth to share the double. Our beds had duvet covers that had been brought over from our home in Kassel. In those days this was unheard of. Most British people only used blankets, but we were used to duvet covers and couldn't sleep without them.

Occasionally when Paula, who at that time was working in a munitions factory, came back after a long evening shift, she would slip into the warm space left by Ruth, who would leave for work very early in the morning. Ruth, at the age of fourteen, had started work in a dress factory. When my mother came in to wake me to get ready for school, she would sometimes mistake Paula for me, and shake her until she woke. Needless to say, whenever this happened, she wasn't happy.

The other bedroom was shared by Jessie and her sister Ethel. Their brothers, Benny, Monty and David, had the bedroom on the half landing. David, the youngest brother, was still at home, but the other two brothers were in the army and only came home on leave periodically. Ethel had a fiancée in the navy, who would spend a lot of time in the house with both families whenever he was on leave.

A PERIOD OF CALM

Even though the bombing of London continued, North London was spared the intensity of the attacks as there was nothing locally of strategic importance for the Germans to target. The Docks in the East End of London had made it a prime target, and the local area had suffered for that. Now that I think about our location, Alexandra Palace was only about a mile and a half away from our house in Crouch End and may have been of interest, as it was used at that time by the British Broadcasting Service. In 1936, the first television programmes came from there. My friends and I used to go there to play, as it was surrounded by some lovely parkland and the most spectacular views of the city.

By this time my brother Jack had started work in the garment district of West London, somewhere near Oxford Street. Although he had primarily studied art and design in Berlin, he had also trained as a window dresser. This meant that Jack, Paula and Ruth were all contributing to the household finances, as was expected of children in those days.

Jack's job came with many perks. One of which was that he would bring home different types of belts and other accessories for us to make up for the garments his firm produced. This gave us another means of income. We used to sit together in the evening, listening to the radio, making up whatever it was that he had brought home for us that day.

Paula had attended a dressmaking and design course prior to leaving Kassel, and was a very talented dressmaker. She was skilful enough to make the most beautiful underwear with complex, intricate designs. As everything was rationed, including clothing, which you could only buy if you had clothing coupons, her skill was highly appreciated by the family. The only fabric that was widely available was Blackout material. This was used to line curtains so that no light could be seen coming from houses during the night, when the German bombers would be on the lookout for any sign of civilisation. When I was a member of a group of country dancers and required a skirt, the only material we could use was Blackout material, which Paula brightened up for me with a coloured braid. It was actually quite a pretty skirt.

Mrs Weinberg was an excellent knitter. As part of the war effort, we were encouraged to knit all sorts of items including scarves, gloves and socks. Wool was provided for us by the local community centre. Mrs Weinberg taught me how to knit, and we spent hours sat in the living room knitting with the radio on in the background. In later years, especially during the 1970s, when knitted garments became fashionable, I produced some lovely knitted suits and coats. I am particularly proud of an oatmeal full-length coat in an Arran design that I still have to this day.

My father began to buy and sell jewellery in Hatton Garden. My grandfather had run a small jewellery repair business in Kassel, so my father, despite having spent most of his life running the menswear business, he also had a reasonably refined knowledge of the jewellery business.

There were so many Jewish refugees trying to make a living at that time. Often they would go to a café on Greville Street and trade together. It didn't take long for my father to build a solid reputation as an honest and astute business man, allowing him to rent an office in Leather Lane and build up his business.

JUNIOR SCHOOL

Eventually, as my English had improved, I started junior school. I think my quick progress was largely down to my love of reading. There was a Boots the Chemist store that had a library on Crouch End High Street. For one penny you could borrow a book for a week. So I borrowed lots of titles of all different genres on a regular basis. I became such an avid reader that my parents had to frequently stop me from reading at the dinner table and set me a rule that I couldn't read any of my library books until I had finished all of my homework. I enjoyed the school except for a few girls who used to bully me because I spoke with an accent.

The school itself was about a mile and a half away from our house. By that time I was used to going out alone and went off each day dutifully. One day, during the winter, my journey was crudely interrupted by a man cycling along   passed by me. As his bicycle rushed past, he rang his bell frantically to get my attention. When I looked over towards him I saw that, up on his handlebar, he had exposed himself! When I arrived at school, I told my girlfriends all about this strange incident. We engaged in a long discussion to figure out why anyone would do such a thing. We were pretty innocent. Even though I had brothers, neither of them ever walked around without wearing underpants.

I remained very innocent throughout my childhood and early adolescence. Aged around eleven or twelve, I remember asking my sisters, "Where do babies come from?", only to receive the rather unhelpful response, "You will find out later!" Jack once brought home a book called *My Life and Loves*, by Frank Harris, which alluded to certain matters that my siblings felt too sordid for their little sister. I once heard them all whispering in the kitchen, agreeing that on no account could they show me the contents of this mysterious book. Of course, this spiked my interest even further. As I hid behind the door, I heard the oven door quickly open and shut. As soon as they had retired from their secret rendezvous, a shrewd little Margot headed straight for the oven and found *My Life and Loves* stashed away like forbidden contraband. I blindly devoured the pages but, in truth, was too young and innocent to really understand what was being described.

During these formative years, one other story stands out in my memory. I had always wanted a small dog. My dream came true on my eleventh birthday, when my parents surprised me with a small mongrel puppy. Sadly, after a few weeks, the dog was hit by a cyclist, and one of his legs was severely injured. The veterinary surgeon tried to save him but was not able to do so. We had to have him put down. I cried solidly for two days and, from that moment on, have never wanted another pet.

HORNSEY HIGH

I was determined not to go to the senior school as I would have had to put up with that same group of girls, who would have made my life unbearable. So I worked hard and earned a scholarship to the local grammar school, Hornsey High School. Several of my friends from my class also made the cut and started there at the same time as me. Because of this, the transition to secondary school was not at all difficult.

I became friends with a girl called Joyce Care, who lived five houses away from me. She had also won a scholarship to Hornsey High. We walked to school together every morning and quickly became good friends. Her mother was a dressmaker and made some really nice dresses for me. Her father worked at the Waterman's ink factory. When we started school, she and I were the same height. In all the years that have passed I may have only grown about another inch, standing at five feet two inches, but Joyce blossomed and ended up growing to five feet ten inches. She was a brilliant tennis player, and I believe met her husband at a tennis club.

The school was very strict when it came to our appearance. We were always expected to wear our uniforms and hats to school, and, if we didn't arrive turned out appropriately, the prefects would report us. As I write this an image comes to mind of the navy knickers that were part of the outfit.

I loved going to school and got good grades but, perhaps more importantly, I found the work interesting and stimulating. I have always had a thirst for knowledge that has stuck with me to this day. I would go into the library after class had finished and ingest as much information as possible whilst leafing through the school's collection of encyclopaedias. In the present, this knowledge comes in handy when playing Trivial Pursuit.

The teachers were a motley crew. Most were quite old. I think the reason for this was that most young women had been assigned a full-time role helping out with the war effort. Many educated young women had been conscripted into the Services. The rest were working either in the land army or in munitions factories.

I remember that the head mistress, Miss Keating, a tiny woman of fifty years or so, shared a flat with the PE teacher, Miss Knight, and that neither of them took kindly to me. My pet hate was PE. I wasn't capable of mastering the various bits of equipment in the gym. Miss Knight, a tall thin grey-haired woman, seemed to take great pleasure from seeing me flounder in the gymnasium. The whole thing made me feel very inadequate. I enjoyed netball and tennis, so all was not lost.

The science teacher, Miss Houseman, reminded me of Queen Victoria as an old woman. She wore a full-length black skirt and her hair was pulled back into a tight bun. In those days we took Latin as a subject. Our Latin teacher was one of the only young teachers. I always admired her beautiful, knitted angora sweaters.

My favourite subjects were history, geography, biology, English literature, the sciences and French. I was very poor at mathematics. At a young age, I had some aspiration to be a pharmacist but was unable to grasp the intricacies of algebra that I believe were necessary for going into that sort of profession.

As Hornsey High School was an all-girls' school, we were taught domestic science, and, as it was wartime, the hockey fields had been ploughed up and were used for gardening lessons. Growing vegetables was a subject that I excelled in. This marked the beginning of my love of gardening, something which has never left me. It was my favourite subject. At home, Mr Weinberg grew vegetables in the garden and kept some chickens. He set aside a small plot for me, where I could practise growing flowers and vegetables with the skills I was learning at school.

Aged about thirteen, I believe I had a crush on a sixth form student called Lola, who had the most beautiful figure, red hair and was a talented artist. At that time I was quite tubby, no doubt from eating too many jam sandwiches.

THE LITTLE BLITZ

In February 1944, the German bombardment intensified and launched a brief but devastating assault on London. The attack became known as the "Little Blitz". By this time the German air force were using buzz-bombs, which made a distinctive rattling noise as they rushed through the air down toward their target. Although this noise was frightfully sinister, it gave you a few moments warning to prepare yourself for the impending attack. You immediately tried to find some shelter if outdoors. If you were indoors then the guidelines were to get under a table in case the house collapsed. In a strange way, living like this didn't seem to frighten me at the age of thirteen or fourteen. I am sure there were times, on hearing the air raid sirens, when I was worried, but, as everyone around me was going through the same experiences and adapting to them, it seemed relatively normal.

Soon the V1 flying bombs were replaced by the far more frightening V2 flying rockets. These were proper rockets. They were much larger and more destructive and gave no little notice of their arrival. There is no doubt that these missiles caused a great deal of damage in London within the short space of a few weeks, causing many casualties and deaths.

One morning, my father was on his way to his office in Hatton Garden when a plate glass window from a large department store suddenly exploded in front of him onto the pavement. The explosion had been caused by a V2 rocket landing on a meat market called Smithfield; an event that resulted in multiple deaths and serious injuries.

Due to the danger of the V2 rocket attacks, my school was closed. It was decided that Ruth and I, as well as my sister-in-law, Jessie, Ethel her sister, and their babies would go up north to get away from London.

A SECOND EVACUATION

I don't know how we ended up in County Durham in the North of England, but I guess someone must have known somebody in the area. Ruth and I were billeted with the manager of a coal mine in a village called East Rainton. Jessie, Ethel and the babies were billeted at the local pub, also in the same village.

It was summer time, and I really enjoyed the environment. East Rainton was a typical English country village, surrounded by huge areas of farm land and greenery wherever you looked. The other interesting characteristic of the village were the large number of pit ponies, which were stabled above ground near the mine.

The manager (I have to refer to him as that as I cannot recall his name) and his wife were lovely people. The main thing I recall from that time was Sunday high tea. What a feast! Our landlady spent all of Sunday morning baking for the week. On these wonderful mornings the smell of baking wafted enticingly through the house. She made scones; pies, both savoury and sweet; and, my favourite, onion tart.

Unlike my previous experience of being evacuated, there was a warm friendly atmosphere here. I think this was because we had grown up significantly since our last experience of evacuation, which meant that it was easier for us to adapt to our new home.

One day, the manager asked Ruth and me whether we would like to experience what it was like down the coal mine. Naturally, we were very curious. He took us to a mine shaft, where we ended up crawling down a tunnel that was only three feet high. I would be lying if I said that I wasn't scared. When I think of the current health and safety guidelines we have in place these days, I look back and reflect on the adventures I would have missed if the same laws were in force at that time.

As Jessie and Ethel had been billeted at the local pub, we often went over there to see them. When it was busy at the weekend, the Landlord asked Ruth to help out serving behind the bar. She was about seventeen at the time. I was also allowed to help but was too young to serve alcohol. I was put to work washing up in the kitchen.

For fun we went to the local village hall, whenever they had dances on, and always had a great time. Ruth was a very beautiful girl, with a gorgeous figure. As I have said, I was a bit tubby at that time. We were lucky to have some really nice dresses to wear, as Aunt Fanny, my mother's sister, used to send us Red Cross parcels from New York, where she was now living with Uncle Isi. They had left Paris as soon as the Nazis had invaded France. These parcels were always something to look forward to, as Aunt Fanny had the most exquisite taste in clothing and only ever wore the latest cuts from the most fashionable designers.

We remained in Durham for several months, visiting Whitby Bay and often venturing into Durham city. I was so happy there that I wanted to stay longer and go to school in Durham. At the end of summer, things had settled down back home, and so we returned to London.

GOLDERS GREEN

School started again in September, but, for some reason, I wasn't as motivated with my school work as I had previously been. As the risk of conflict on these shores had begun to calm down as the allied troops had invaded Europe, my parents decided it was time for us to find our own house. They quickly found a suitable property in North West London, Golders Green, and decided to buy.

The move to Golders Green was seen as a big achievement for the family in terms of becoming upwardly mobile. It was a lovely house in the Ridgeway, in a turning parallel to the main Golders Green Road. The accommodation consisted of two reception rooms, a large kitchen and five bedrooms over two floors. It was a 1920s build. One of the reception rooms had wood panelling; whilst the other leading to the garden was very light and airy. The dining room furniture was made by Epstein, who, at that time, was very much in vogue. The designs were Art Deco and of the 1930s Bauhaus style. The house was furnished with tables and sideboards made of blonde wood, leather sofas and armchairs with wooden trimmings.

We once again had a radio, a gramophone and a large collection of 78rpm vinyl records that catered for all our tastes, including a wide variety of classical artists of that era and a selection for us girls consisting of Bing Crosby, Harry James, Stan Kenton and a number of other popular artists of the time.

CINEMA

Ruth and I usually went to the cinema at least once a week. We loved all the film stars of that era, in particular Humphrey Bogart and Ingrid Bergman. We enjoyed musicals with Gene Kelly and Doris Day, comedy with Abbot and Costello and adored all the glamorous women like Rita Hayworth and Betty Grable.

The cinema was undoubtedly the highlight of the week. With no television, cinema was the most accessible form of escapism for the general public. Of course, I have always loved to read, but it didn't compare to the wonders of the silver screen, which could transport you from the austerity of wartime London to the glamour and glitz of Hollywood ballrooms and private parties. For me, it was all about the romanticism of Hollywood. These stars always moved so gracefully as if walking on air. They conducted themselves with such elegance at all times and spoke with a wit and sophistication that simply isn't matched by what we see in the cinema of the present day with its over-reliance on special effects. The male leads were always so handsome and, for those days, the spectacle was surprisingly sexually charged.

It was also a time of adolescent awareness for me. Ruth educated me to the seamier side of life, especially warning me about certain men who would try to feel your leg in the cinema whilst you were looking up at the screen. She said that I had a choice if I ever felt someone touching me. I could move to another seat, if the cinema was not too full, or just pinch his hand as hard as I could. She said the harder I pinched the faster he would move away. It was great advice and always worked. Younger readers might be surprised by how often these advances needed to be rebuked. You simply wouldn't get away with that kind of behaviour today. Instead of a pinch, these men would end up in prison.

AFTER THE WAR

In the spring of 1945, victory in Europe was declared. Ruth and Paula went to Trafalgar Square to join in the celebrations. My parents didn't allow me to accompany them as they felt I was too young. Even though there was a wonderful sense of jubilation, it was impossible to get away from the fact that fathers, sons and husbands hadn't yet returned, a lot of whom would never return.

As the troops advanced through Europe, the newsreels began showing the devastation of the war and the impact of the destruction on the countries involved. The worst images came from the concentration camps. These images were almost unanimously met with disbelief. The atrocities committed by the Nazis were so horrendous that people couldn't comprehend what had really happened.

It was an issue of disassociation. All of sudden the public were being shown images of people so severely emaciated and downtrodden that they looked more like skeletons than any living human beings that they had ever come across. At first the horror and reality of these images didn't register with them, and they were simply unable to believe what it was they were seeing. It didn't make any sense to them. For us these pictures hit home immediately. We had left family behind in Kassel and, at that time, had no way of knowing what had happened to them.

When the weather was warm, we spent a lot of time in the kitchen as there were large patio doors leading out into the garden. One day, whilst sitting there listening to the radio, there was an announcement regarding the dropping of the atomic bomb on 6 August, 1945. On this occasion, I definitely didn't comprehend the full implications of what the announcement was telling me, at least not until I went to the cinema and saw the newsreels showing the extent of the damage caused.

In those days, because the news was relayed via radio or newspapers, the events described were difficult to understand unless you saw them on a weekly newsreel. In the twenty-first century, we have twenty-four hour non-stop coverage of world events that can be viewed on iphones, ipads, computers and other devices. At times, our senses become overloaded with information. I often feel disturbed by the way that this constant repetition can disassociate you from the grim reality of the events depicted on screen.

Of course, the events of that day, the destruction of Hiroshima and Nagasaki, have been well documented and led to the surrender of the Japanese army. It was the end to the war in the Far East.

Golders Green at that time was seen as a desirable area to live, especially for London's thriving Jewish population. There was a large synagogue, as well as many shops catering for Orthodox Jews. There was also a great transport system, and it was close to Hampstead Heath and Highgate Woods for outings.

My father was very content in his new home. One of the smaller rooms was used as his office, and every day, when he returned home, he would lock himself away in there to do his accounts. My father was utterly dedicated to the keeping of the books, applying the utmost care, precision and discipline, even to the smallest change he had in his pocket. It was just another practice of his that made him a successful business man and helped a great deal in keeping the family on top of its monetary worries during these hard times.

Socially, great changes were occurring in the UK. The shortages continued. The conservative government lost the elections and Clement Attlee and his Labour party introduced major changes. It remained a time of great austerity. Great rebuilding programmes were starting to rehouse the huge number of people that had lost their homes during the various episodes of bombing and rocket attacks.

In Europe millions of people had been displaced and the horror of the concentration camps became very real, as families tried to trace loved ones only to be told that they had perished at Auschwitz, at Dachau, at Treblinka. People who had survived the camps joined up with their relatives and appeared determined to reclaim life again. I met many people during that time who had survived. They were so focused on living life to the full, as if they were doing so on behalf of those who had not been as fortunate as them.

My grandfather died in the Theresienstat concentration camp. One of my aunts, a cousin, who was the same age as me, and his sister, who was the same age as Ruth, all died in Auschwitz.

My maternal grandmother, who had been living in Paris with my Aunty Marie, died during the German occupation. She had to remain in Paris when my aunty had left for the South of France, as she had been quite elderly.

The summer of 1947 was a particularly hot summer in England. As we now had a fairly large garden, we could sit out there to sunbathe. In our kitchen, there were a variety of bottles including some tanning lotions standing on a shelf for our use. Unlike my sisters I was very fair skinned, and it took quite a few sessions for me to go from semi-burnt to a light, tan colour. My sisters, on the other hand, became tropical beauties overnight.

This leads to a funny story involving my father. One Saturday that summer, when I was probably about sixteen years old, my mother and I went out shopping for a few hours, a favourite pastime of ours. My father was home from work and was making the most of the good weather by relaxing in the garden reading the newspaper. On our return, as we entered the kitchen, we noticed a strong smell of furniture polish and couldn't make any sense of it. My father was very much a man of his time; it was unheard of for a husband to help his wife out with the cleaning.

When he heard us return, he came in from the garden. We were at once overwhelmed by the smell of furniture polish. He said he had been feeling very warm out in the sun and, as he did not wish to burn, had picked up one of the bottles of, what he thought, was suntan lotion. He had not looked carefully enough at the labels and, as all the creams looked the same to him, had accidently picked up the wrong one and had applied several thick layers of furniture polish to his shoulders, neck and cheeks. We were naturally very amused by this incident, and it became one of the stories we told over and over again at family gatherings. Before you judge my father as being completely useless, I should remind you that my father had severely damaged his sense of smell as a small child.

On a side note, it was around this time, perhaps in early 1947, that I caught the flu which resulted in a metamorphosis from Margot, the tubby teenager, to Margot, the slender young woman.

DANCING AND DATING

As my education had been disrupted, the prospect of starting a new school didn't appeal to me. My parents suggested that, if I didn't wish to continue with my grammar school education, I needed to start working toward an occupation. I was enrolled into Pitman's College in Ballard's Lane, North London, and began to train as a secretary.

I was fifteen years old when I started the eighteen-month course. It was quite comprehensive and included classes on shorthand, touch-typing, bookkeeping and general office duties. I was also required to learn yet another language. The skills learnt, all that time ago, have continued to prove useful to this day, as I still touch-type when using my computer.

During my time at Pitman's, I made a number of good friends. It was with these girlfriends that I began to go to dances and started to really enjoy my teenage years.

I loved dancing. Every weekend my friend Rae and I, sometimes joined by other friends, would go to dances organised by different Jewish social clubs in venues all over the West End of London. Occasionally, we also went to some of the more popular dance halls that were in fashion at the time, such as the Astoria, the Lyceum and the Hammersmith Palace. Sometimes we went to tea dances in hotels, like the Regent Palace Hotel, the Cumberland Hotel and the Piccadilly Hotel.

I wasn't yet allowed to go out on a date on my own, so I had to condense all of my flirting into the hours spent at these venues. All that I really wanted was to be asked to dance and, as I was a pretty young thing, I was lucky not to have to sit out on many dances.

Sometimes my friends and I would go to a movie and then afterwards move on to Lyons Corner House for supper. Our favourite place to eat was the Salad Bowl, where for five shillings we could help ourselves to as much food as we wanted. Austerity measures were still in place, so the most one could spend on a meal out was five shillings, which converted into present money works out at about twenty-five pence.

Once or twice, my friends and I organised a weekend trip to Brighton. We would go dancing at Sherry's, a very popular dancehall down there by the coast.

When I left Pitman's College, I was in a position to start looking for work. My girlfriends all managed to get various secretarial positions, but my parents decided that it would be better for me to work for my father in his office in Hatton Garden. This news filled me with mixed emotions. I was definitely apprehensive about working for a stranger, but, by taking that option, I would have earned a decent living. One of my friends was earning £3.50 a week, which seemed like a lot of money compared to what I would make working in my father's office. My father offered me fifteen shillings per week, because I was living at home. I could keep that as my pocket money.

"Why work for strangers?" he said.

As usual Margot, the good girl, agreed. I began working in Hatton Garden on a daily basis. I did the bookkeeping, typed any letters, packed parcels, went to the post office and, on occasion, delivered goods to local customers.

The years spent in our lovely house in Golders Green were good years. My father's business continued to thrive, both my sisters married and I continued to enjoy my teenage years, going to parties and dances with my friends.

MARGOT AND HER SISTERS

Paula met her husband through an indirect introduction of a business colleague of my father. She told him that her son was in the air force stationed in Africa and would love to have a female pen pal. So the correspondence began.

There was an amusing twist to this. Paula didn't have a sufficient knowledge of written English at the time, so Ruth helped her write these letters. There was a running joke in our family that Len, Paula's future husband, had inadvertently fallen in love with Ruth, as she had been the one whose words and handwriting he had become so fond of.

When they finally met, Paula and Len fell in love and, as both families approved, got engaged and married in the early part of 1947. It was a fairly large wedding with lots of relatives from both sides of the family and many friends in attendance. Ruth and I were bridesmaids, a very exciting experience. The reception was held in Churchill's night club on Bond Street.

I continued to go dancing and, as Paula had now married, Ruth would ask me whether I would join her occasionally. Now that I was sixteen, she felt it was acceptable for me to accompany her when her girlfriends were unavailable. It was during one of these Saturday night dances at the Brent Bridge Hotel, not too far away from where we were living in Golders Green and the same hotel that the World Cup winning English football team stayed in 1966, that she met her husband to be, Leon Hartman. He had recently been discharged after serving as an engineer in the British army, where he had spent some time in Italy as well as other countries while the army advanced through Europe. He was ten years older than Ruth and was ready to settle down.

Ruth and Leon married in January 1948. This was a time of great austerity in England, and power cuts were frequent during that winter. In fact, during their wedding reception, at the Brent Bridge Hotel, there was a power cut. Fortunately, the reception continued in candlelight, which worked out to be a blessing in disguise as it created the most romantic of moods.

As there was a housing shortage, Paula and her husband were living with us in the family house, as we had two spare rooms on the second floor of our house. This changed when Ruth married. My father helped with a deposit on a house in Finchley Road, Golders Green, and the two couples, both my sisters and their husbands, divided the house into two flats and shared the accommodation.

So, my two sisters were married; my eldest brother was married; Herman was in Detroit; and the youngest child was left at home.

CHAPTER THREE 1949-1951

AN AMERICAN DREAM

The year was 1949. I was eighteen years old and moving to America. The most exciting aspect of the whole adventure was that we would be living in Los Angeles. The anticipation was almost too much to bear. The prospect of living in a city so deeply rooted in the movies and show business filled me with an immense delight. I couldn't wait to immerse myself in all the glamour, dancing and sunshine. Of course, the celluloid images of Hollywood shown in London cinemas in the 1940s had left me with many preconceived ideas of what to expect, much of which had been exaggerated both originally in the film studio and then by me in my own dreams and fantasies. Before I get ahead of myself, I must disclose some precursory information as to how it is that our family moved to the States.

When we were trying to escape Kassel my parents had submitted a visa application to move to America, but it didn't get processed in time. As both of them had been born in Poland, their submission was treated as part of the Polish quota, for which the waiting list was known to be significantly longer. Following *Kristallnacht*, the sudden increase in the severity of the situation forced my parents' hand. They simply couldn't afford to wait any longer. We packed up our belongings and came to England. But, in terms of the formalities, everything was now sorted; our application had been received in the States and all the papers were in place. There wasn't much in the way to stop us from moving across to that side of the Atlantic.

I don't know what made them come to this decision as we were very settled in England. My father's business was flourishing, my parents were happy within their social circle, Ruth and Paula were both married, as was my brother Jack, and they had several grandchildren. Herman, who was now living in New York, and myself were the only single children left to marry off.

In 1947, my parents had visited my uncle in Detroit and must have enjoyed their sojourn. In all likelihood, it was the lifestyle in the United States that appealed to them. Austerity was very much the name of the game in the UK and it continued to be throughout the 1950s. At the same time, America was enjoying a post-war boom of mass consumer culture.

Unlike my first experience of migration, which was clouded in an oppressive atmosphere of anxiety and fear, the migration to the US was a most enjoyable affair. The two experiences couldn't have been more contrasting. The whole thing was sufficiently planned and well organised, and I had a large part to play in this.

In preparation for the move, we had to sit through several meetings and undertake a whole host of medical tests at the American Embassy in Grosvenor Square. During these meetings I took on the role of family spokeswoman, as my parents, despite speaking excellent English, felt that, when it came to dealing with officials, they needed all the help they could get in case they misunderstood anything. In retrospect, I think my parents' previous experience with bureaucracy in Nazi Germany had made them particularly wary of government officials. As the main part of my education had taken place in England, my English was almost perfect. By that time I am sure I was even thinking in English.

We undertook a full medical examination including x-rays and blood tests. This was my first encounter with these medical procedures and I have to admit that I was terrified by the sight of the nurse's syringe filing up with my blood. I became dizzy and nearly passed out.

My brother Herman had come over from America to help us with the move. As soon as our house was sold, we once again found ourselves on a journey into the unknown.

THE BOAT TRIP

We left London on a train from Waterloo Station headed for Southampton. When the train pulled into the station, which was situated on the waterfront right in the middle of the docks, I stepped off the train and was instantly immersed in all the hustle and bustle of the port. In front of me stood the magnificent ship that would be transporting us to our new home. It was the legendary Queen Mary, the original model.

There were lots of people milling around anxiously at the dockside saying their goodbyes and embracing their loved ones. I was struck by a feeling of great unease. The idea of leaving my sisters and brother and their respective families transformed from a distant, superficial impression into a cruel, immediate reality. Many tears were shed. Unlike today, when a plane journey can whisk you around the world in a matter of hours, global transportation was a slow and onerous process. We knew that it would be a long time until we saw each other again. Travel was a major event in those days, especially for a family with our recent history.

I looked around with interest at my fellow passengers, taking note of those who were going on board. There were different classes for the various passengers: first class, cabin class and third class. We were situated in cabin class. Once on board, the different classes were sectioned off from each other and moving amongst passengers of a different class was impossible. The British class system was still very much in full force at that time.

There was so much to absorb on board, too much. This abundance of novel experiences, sea sickness being one of the least pleasant, meant that I was so thoroughly caught up in the moment, entranced, that everything became a bit of a blur. I do not have any clear memories of us actually setting sail. All I am left with is a residual sense of general excitement and joy. But this was just the first of many new experiences I was to encounter in the next few months.

As an eighteen-year-old, I was very conscious that there were hardly any young people on board. There were a couple of young men that I recognised, as I had seen them performing dance routines at the London Palladium. Herman, who was far more confident than me, initiated a conversation with them and we all became quite friendly over the duration of the crossing. It impressed me greatly that I had spoken to people who were in show business.

A humorous episode occurred when I went to my brother's cabin to pick up a book he had borrowed. Herman had black hair and very dark eyes and was a very handsome young man. As I had blonde hair and blue eyes, we didn't look much like brother and sister, so the steward's reaction was not wholly unexpected. I was knocking on his door as a steward happened to pass by. This steward, adding two and two together to make five, gave me what can only be described as a knowing look. I quickly tried to explain what was really going on by saying that it was my brother's room, but, just as I spoke, Herman opened the door and asked me to come in. The steward winked at him and went off smiling to himself.

We had a very pleasant crossing as it was July, and the weather was fabulous. I spent a lot of time on deck sunbathing and playing cards with some of the few young people on board.

As with every other immigrant approaching New York over the past century, I watched in awe as the Statue of Liberty grew larger and larger and the skyline of Manhattan lingered flirtatiously on the horizon. Again, this was something I had previously seen in the movies and now it was right there in front of me.

NEW YORK

New York in July was hot, humid and perpetually noisy. The wailing sirens of police cars, ambulances and fire tenders were a permanent feature. I had never experienced a city so animated. In London, the blitz had really taken its toll on the people and the architecture. In comparison, New York was an entirely different breed of city. This was epitomised by the scenes at Times Square where the famous neon lights seemed more like a caricature than a real life setting.

My mother and I went out shopping, paying particular attention to the dress shops and the variety and selection of clothing on offer. As there had been great austerity in England both during the war and after it, we were used to getting by on clothing coupons. To be able to wander through these shops with no restriction was like stumbling into Aladdin's cave. Needless to say, I ended up with a number of lovely dresses that were more suited to the current climate.

We stayed in New York for three weeks on the fourteenth floor of a hotel. I had never lived at such an altitude. Although the view was incredible, the realisation that we were so high up was a constant source of discomfort, and I was terrified to look out or stand too close to the windows. During stormy weather, the thunder sounded like cannon fire and echoed between the skyscrapers.

My brother had been working in New York for a while as he had been invalided out of the United States Army following an accident to his knee in training. I really enjoyed getting to know him after all those years, as I had had very little contact with him up to that point. He had now been living in America for eleven years, having left Germany for the States as a fourteen-year-old boy. Herman had since become a handsome twenty-five-year-old man with an outgoing, jovial personality. Because of this he had many friends, who he introduced me to during those few weeks in New York. I took an enormous amount of pleasure going out with his friends on many fun evenings. I enjoyed meeting one of his friends in particular, a very handsome Italian American/Jewish friend, who I think was interested in me as he continued to write to me when we moved on to Los Angeles. I enjoyed the attention, but had other things on my mind. I was much more focused on the next step of my American adventure.

ON THE ROAD

As I have said, New York wasn't our final destination. Although it would have been a fantastic place to stay, there was a lot more of America to explore. The temptation to move on was impossible to resist. Even Herman packed up his things and came along with us. In fact, he drove us. Our plan was to drive across America to LA. Our first port of call was to see my father's brother, who was still living in Detroit. My father hadn't seen much of his brother over the last twenty years. They had only seen each other once, when my parents had visited a few years earlier.

My Uncle Harry had settled in Detroit during the 1920s after living in the Mid-West, where he had attempted to live as a real-life cowboy. He had married a lady who had been born in Russia. They had four children and ran a garage business. I met my three male cousins, but didn't meet my cousin Bernice until we arrived in Los Angeles, where she was living with her husband, Darwin. Bernice and Darwin had decided to settle there after the war, in which he had served as a pilot in the US Air Force. It was an absolute delight to meet these American cousins of ours. The eldest was married, the second son was twenty-two and a pharmacist, and the youngest, Seymour, was fifteen. Bernice must have been about twenty-four at the time.

On leaving Detroit, we stopped off at all sorts of fabulous destinations. In all, it took us just over six weeks to make our way across to Los Angeles. On the road, my mood varied between the joy of seeing all the amazing places that we passed and a capricious teenage petulance. For instance, this grotty, moody teenager refused to take a swim and float in the Great Salt Lake. I think the constant proximity of my parents was all too much for me, as it would have been for many teenagers, and also made me aware that I was missing my friends that I had left in England. So, in spite of how incredible the whole travelling experience was, I would often descend into an almighty sulk.

The place that made the greatest impression on me was the Grand Canyon. We had been to Yellowstone Park, Bryce Canyon, Denver, and they were all impressive sights; however, for me they didn't compare to the Grand Canyon. Remember that it was more than sixty years ago. Travel was not as commercialised as it is now, meaning there were hardly any other tourists around. The only building in sight was a small motel at the edge of the canyon.

There were no helicopters or planes flying around, just complete silence. The vastness of the silence was matched by the enormity of the scenery itself, which glistened with intense, violent colouring. The size of it was too much for one person to take in. I wrote to all my friends trying to share these sights with them, but I knew that my effort was in vain. I was aware that it was necessary to experience this wonderful sight to understand the nature of its beauty. In the present, I have promised myself a trip back to the Grand Canyon as I want to walk out onto the glass platform that has recently been completed.

We continued our journey through the Mohave Desert, driving in a car without air conditioning. As a precaution, every single car that entered the dessert was equipped with water bags in order to top up their radiators. The heat was exceptional, almost unbearable.

We stopped at Las Vegas, which at that time consisted of just three hotels. I have been back at various times since then. Each visit I am amazed about how much it continues to develop. I view Las Vegas as the equivalent of Disneyland for grown-ups in the sense that it is a fantasy land that I quickly tire of after a few days.

Eventually, we arrived in Los Angeles. Now that our journey was over, I became a little anxious about building a new life and making new friends. I had to learn so much about this new city and this foreign land. Regardless, I continued to enjoy all the challenges this migration threw at me. It really helped me to mature, and I will never regret that my parents decided to move to America.

WEST OLYMPIC BOULEVARD

My parents found what is now called a new build. A beautiful modern apartment, which was one of four, situated on 5550 West Olympic Boulevard. These boulevards in Los Angeles led all the way from downtown LA to the beach at Santa Monica.

My mother and I had a great time furnishing the apartment. My parents had decided that I shouldn't go to work, but keep my mother company. So off we went looking at all kinds of wonderful modern furniture. This might be how I developed my love of line and colour, but on reflection it was just something that ran in the family. Jack had attended art school, Paula attended a dressmaking school and Ruth was able to produce the most beautiful designs for any style of dress, whether it was for her three daughters or for her own formal ball gowns.

The kitchen was amazingly modern, with built-in appliances, a garbage disposal unit and an ironing board that retracted into the kitchen wall. It was California living at its most modern. Our lounge had a green and mauve sofa, amongst other contemporary accessories of that era.

Exploring Los Angeles, particularly going to the beach at Santa Monica, was great fun. As always, I was determined to get a great sun tan, so smothered myself in a mix of baby oil and iodine. It was many years before the dangers of excessive sun exposure became widely acknowledged. But, as Bernard Shaw said:

"Youth is a wonderful thing, what a crime it is to waste it on the young."
– Bernard Shaw

After a few months of this lifestyle, I was beginning to feel that I should make use of the training I had received at Pitman's College and managed to get a position as a secretary in a reform synagogue opposite to where we lived. This was just a part-time position though, as the woman who I was replacing was only away on sick leave. I thoroughly enjoyed working there and was able to run the office without any problems. I think I enjoyed, what was for me, the novelty of the role, although, I have never felt comfortable working in an office based environment with a nine-to-five type of employment.

In retrospect, at the age of eighteen, it would have been a good idea to go to university. If I had taken this option, I would probably have enrolled at UCLA. In America almost everyone went to university. There were two issues that prevented me. The first was a lack of self confidence in my ability to undertake a university education. Despite always achieving excellent results at grammar school, I lacked the confidence to return to education. The second was that in my family girls were expected to be married by the time they were twenty.

For large parts of my life, I have been enrolled on courses in the adult education sector. My first go at this was in LA. The course I attended there was called "Radio Voice" and taught me how to speak on the radio. Television had not yet kicked off and so radio programmes were very popular. I think I must have aspired to become an actress in radio plays.

I have always had an innate curiosity and thirst for learning. I have a belief that anything we learn in our life will never be wasted and will often be of use in furthering other learning.

For as long as I can remember, I have had a need to prove to my parents that I was capable of earning my own income without having to rely on the family. My parents always preferred for their children to help out with the family business. There is an underlying theme through my story of me looking for projects that would show my parents how capable I was of working for myself. However, on many occasions in my earlier years the good girl in me was quick to adhere to my father's wishes and follow the path that he had laid down for me. This prevented me from becoming fully emancipated for many years.

MAKING FRIENDS

My mother was aware that I was quite shy and lacking in confidence, so suggested that I attended a course at a finishing school, a place where one learned to be "charming". This included learning things like how to sit and walk correctly, how to apply cosmetics correctly, being able to converse appropriately and how to appear poised in all manner of situations. We even attended classes on fencing, as it was supposed to encourage us to become more graceful. This course seemed to give me the upward jolt in confidence that I needed, and to this day I haven't forgotten and still use some of the techniques that I learnt there.

It was by following the suggestion of the course director that I took part in some photographic modelling for catalogues specialising in shorter women. It was quite fun, but not really that fulfilling. Herman had a friend who was an aspiring photographer and worked in a photographic shop in Beverley Hills. It was this friend who helped me build up a portfolio of glamorous shots to show to the modelling agencies. He really put a lot of effort into the shoots, making sure the photographs came out as professional-looking as possible. I think this was partly down to him taking a fancy for me.

I must admit that I was enchanted by the glamour of Hollywood, the sunshine of California, the beach boys in Santa Monica on Muscle Beach, and the music with big bands such as Harry James and Tommy Dorsey playing music at the Hollywood Palladium. I loved to dance, jitterbugging to all this popular music for hours on end. It was common to finish the evening by going to one of the many drive-through burger restaurants, which were unheard of in England at that time, yet were an integral part of youth culture in California. Another popular past time was going to the drive-in cinemas, where we sat in our cars in an enormous car park in front of a gigantic screen.

I was very much seen as different, as the English girl. This worked to my advantage, and I became very popular because I was a welcome variation from the homogeneous horde of bobby-soxers who went to the University of California. The film *Grease* is a remarkably accurate portrayal of how I remember the atmosphere in Los Angeles during the two years I lived there.

I joined the Jewish youth club that was part of the local synagogue and became acquainted with a delightful girlfriend, Yetty. She was a refugee from Poland, but was living with her brother and sister-in-law in Los Angeles. She was a couple of years older than me and, whilst I was still living out there in Los Angeles, met and fell in love with Mendel Sachs, who later became a renowned academic in the field of theoretical physics continuing the work of Einstein. They married and had three sons.

I was very lucky to find such a great place to make friends. The synagogue was very modern. For instance, men and woman sat together and socialising between sexes was encouraged. To me it always seemed like the synagogue, through its various social clubs and events, was more interested in providing a community than enforcing strict religious practice. I have to say that this suited me perfectly.

As well as Yetty, I became good friends with two really nice girls, Norma and Eleanor. These two girls were true Americans. It was great for me to experience American life and culture with the help of these two knowledgeable guides.

There was a certain distinctive buzz around America at that time. Everyone seemed carefree and happy; no demographic more so than the young. There was a lot of dancing, flirting and all that kind of stuff. Even though I was no stranger to this, as in England we had had our share of fun, it seemed a lot more laid-back and relaxed in America. It always struck me as odd how young men would cruise around in their cars looking to pick up girls and would quite openly drive up to a group of girls on the street and casually try to "get lucky".

One evening we were standing outside a club when a limousine pulled up. From the back seats of this luxury vehicle emerged three young guys, all looking really sharp, if a little suspect, but reasonably handsome. They approached us with such confidence and charm that we chatted with them for quite a while. They asked us if we wanted to go for a ride and that they would take us for a meal or to a night club, whatever we desired. Being a smart group of girls with our heads firmly screwed on, we turned them down politely. But on another night, who knows? They might have convinced us. God knows where we would have ended up if we had taken up their offer. There were a lot of gangster-types in Los Angeles at the time. A young girl had to be careful.

DATING IN AMERICA

I had the usual crushes on guys and was in and out of love as the mood would take me, much like any young girl. Through the club I met a few young men whom I dated. There were also many blind dates that were arranged by my parents and their friends.

I remember one time going on a blind date with a guy who wasn't my usual type. He wasn't particularly handsome and was full of himself; however, he was a syndicated columnist for the *LA Times* and other papers nationwide, writing a popular movie column. This relationship lasted for a few weeks, and I was able to join him at some premieres. He took me to Universal Film Studios and actually introduced me to Bob Hope. I also met the famous Al Jolson and several female stars, such as Debbie Reynolds. These memories are really precious to me, not because of the boyfriend, but because the meetings with all these A-list stars gave me the chance to feel like I was part of the Hollywood scene.

Our brief relationship had an abrupt ending. I rang him on the telephone and his mother answered. Because I didn't know who had answered the phone, I immediately asked if he was in and if I could speak to him. Apparently this was not only a huge faux-pas but an unforgivable offence. His mother instantly disliked me, thinking me as rude. Obviously he was very close to her and in order not too upset her or go against her will he ended things with me. He told me that I hadn't been respectful to his mother and that we couldn't continue to see each other. What a lucky escape! He was obviously a mummy's boy.

There was one man whom I considered as possible husband material. He was a psychologist. Unfortunately, he was slightly too old for me. He was thirty-three and wasn't prepared to settle down for quite a few more years, not until he had completed his analysis. I found him charismatic and delightful, and, by speaking with him, I became interested in psychology. His influence upon me lasted my whole life. I believe the reason that I took psychology as a subject when I returned to study in 1980 was down to the enjoyment I received discussing psychology with him and mixing with his intellectual friends. One New Year's Eve, he took me to a party where I spent the evening socialising with a room full of psychology professors and students. It was an all-night affair with the discussions lasting till five o'clock in the morning. Of course, most of the debate went well over my head, but was nevertheless intriguing.

There was another good looking young man, Greg, who lived in one of the apartments below ours. I remember first seeing him when his family moved in. I was watching from the window and, when I first caught sight of him, was thrilled because he looked Jewish. I became excited about the possibility of having a Jewish young man living close by. Much to my disappointment he was from a Lebanese family, who were very strict Catholics.

My parents had told me that I wasn't allowed to go out with anyone who wasn't of the Jewish faith. It just so happened that his parents had prescribed the same restrictions on him, although tilted toward the catholic persuasion. We became very friendly, but never let any romantic feeling develop despite spending a lot of time together. He did actually ask me out on what could have been interpreted as a date. He had tickets for a Stan Kenton concert. I was keen to take him up on his invitation but my parents intervened and forced me to decline.

HERMAN AND PAULA

My brother Herman was working with my father, who had decided to continue with the jewellery business. He had formed some contacts with a couple of people he knew from London and opened a jewellery shop in downtown Los Angeles. He never really enjoyed working with retail clients and so decided to open a wholesale office in the Jewellery Trades Building, also located downtown. In 1966, when my parents decided to return to London, Herman took over. Herman ran the business until he retired in 2012. At the age of eighty-eight, he felt it was time to retire and have some fun.

In 1950, Herman met a very nice young woman named Florence, a nurse. I think they met through a friend of his and, after a brief courtship, married in the same year.

Around the same time, my sister Paula immigrated to New Zealand with her husband, Len. My brother-in-law had not been able to settle in London after his return from serving in the Air Force and didn't find his trade as a watch maker particularly stimulating. They decided to emigrate in 1950 and visited us in Los Angeles on their way to New Zealand.

When Paula had lived in England, she had been told that it was unlikely she would ever be able to have children, and she and Len had resigned themselves to this. I don't know whether it was the change of air, the southern hemisphere or whether the bath water runs anticlockwise there, but quite soon after they moved out there she became pregnant. In rapid succession she gave birth to four daughters.

I feel that Paula and I never really knew each other. This was mainly down to the eight-year age gap between us. One of her daughters came to England in 1972 and stayed with us for a while, before moving to London. When she married, Paula and Len came over for the wedding and on one further occasion. I have never been to New Zealand so haven't seen them since.

In 2012, she will celebrate her ninetieth birthday, as she was born in 1922.

PARENTS' CONCERN

I think that my parents were becoming concerned that I was going out on too many dates. Whenever I announced that I was going out with someone who my parents didn't know, I was obliged to invite them to our home for an inspection of sorts. My father would inquire about their family background, the business their father was in, their own occupation, their future plans and so on. It was all quite formal. Obviously my parents were worried I might fall for someone that they wouldn't approve of, or even get into "trouble"! They didn't need to worry about any of that, as I had enough sense not to go too far. I recall having to turn down the advances of some of the more eager boyfriends. I would say that that the reason I could resist the temptation was two-fold. First of all, what you don't know you won't miss. Second of all, if I tried it and liked what was offered, I could become addicted and that would be far more serious. This was before the contraceptive pill, and it was important for good girls to be sensible. As a result, we were all probably very frustrated.

At the beginning of 1951, my parents suggested that my mother and I should go to London to visit the family, as she was missing the grandchildren. It was only supposed to be a temporary trip, but I think they hoped I would meet an appropriate man in London and settle down there. This was, in fact, what fate had in store for me. I never returned to live in Los Angeles. My American dream was short-lived, but everything I had hoped it would be.

CHAPTER FOUR 1951-1960

THE FABULOUS FIFTIES

The news was dominated by the immense and perilous rivalry between the US and the Soviet Union that threatened to boil over into all-out nuclear war. An ideological conflict between capitalism and communism spurred on these two super-powers, leading to displays of each nation's military muscle and technological wizardry. Most notably, this was demonstrated by the testing of Nuclear weapons (such as RDS-37 and Upshot-Knothole) and the Space Race. In the US, the Red Scare caused public congressional hearings where Hollywood stars were blacklisted. Away from the Cold War, decolonisation was beginning to be seen throughout Africa and Asia, although it only really accelerated in the 1960s.

My mother and I returned to London in 1951 to visit Ruth and Jack, both of whom had settled in London with their young families. My mother wanted to see her grandchildren, and I was very happy to come along for the journey. Of course, I missed them all too. We flew to New York and then sailed on the Queen Elizabeth to Southampton. It was springtime, and we had a very pleasant crossing despite some choppy weather.

In the 1950s, London was a fabulous city to live in. Coming back to London didn't affect my lifestyle much. Everything continued to move at the same heady pace and with the same sort of buzz that I had experienced in Los Angeles.

TONY

There was an unspoken understanding that, as I had reached my twenties, it was time for me to find a husband and settle down. It was still very acceptable for Jewish families to organise arranged marriages. It wasn't so much an "arranged marriage" in the way that most people understand the term, but more that my parents had to approve of any potential husband, much like they had been doing already with my dates. It worked like my own personal dating service. They would often approach me with the name of a man that they thought would make a good husband. The rest was up to me. I could choose whether to meet the guy or not, and, if I liked him, it was my choice to take things further.

I didn't really know any better, so these restrictions weren't an issue. In fact, it saved me the personal hassle of having to worry whether the men I liked would match up to my parents' ideals, and remember I was always a good girl so I was more than happy to go along with my parents' wishes. I knew that they always had my best interests at heart. So, although I use the term "arranged marriage", it was never the case that I would be forced to marry, or even date, a man who I didn't like or find attractive.

Prior to our move to America, a potential husband had been suggested to me by my parents. It was a business acquaintance of my father who had mentioned to him that he was ready to settle down. His name was Tony, and he was ten years older than me. My mother had always told me that it was better to marry an older man, as he would appreciate me and be settled in his career. I think I went on one date with him back then and found him pleasant enough.

Like my father, Tony was also in the jewellery business. He had come over to England in 1938 to attend the University of Bradford and study textiles. His family came from Lithuania and owned textile and timber mills. His father had trained to be a doctor, but had then gone into the family banking business.

When I first met Tony in 1949, he was aware that his parents had been killed in Belsen concentration camp. It was a very sad story. As the men and women were always separated in the camps, his parents found themselves parted from each other. Once inside Belsen, his mother had managed to locate some of her female friends from her town. One day, whilst making their usual rounds of the women's camp, the guards were asking whether anyone would like to take a brief rest from work. An offer like this, the opportunity for a break, seemed too good to be true. None of her friends volunteered themselves and, when it looked like she might be tempted, warned her against it as no one could tell what the guards would do next. But the work was so unbearably tough that she couldn't resist this chance of a rest. She volunteered to go. The outcome was that she was taken to the gas chambers.

I met her friends after the war, who had survived by doing various jobs in the camp. It was very sad to know that Tony's mother also had this chance to survive.

The only surviving relatives of his were a female cousin and her daughter, who came to live with him when they were freed from Belsen. When they were taken from their home, his cousin's daughter was only thirteen years old. Children of this age were usually sent to the gas chambers as they were deemed too young to cope with the harsh demands of the labour. The cousin's husband and her young son of seven were taken away from them and perished in the gas chambers. When she arrived at the camp, she told the guards that her daughter was sixteen years old, a lie which saved her daughter's life. Consequently, they were both sent to work and were allowed to remain together.

A PRIVILEGED LIFE

As we were back in England and comparatively close to our relatives in continental Europe, my mother wanted to go to Paris to visit her sisters. My mother had two sisters, who had both settled in Paris during the 1930s.

Her younger sister, Fanny, was the one who, with the help of her husband's connections, had arranged our escape from Nazi Germany all those years before. As I have already mentioned, they moved to America during the war, but had since returned to Paris.

The other sister, Marie, was married to a businessman and had one daughter, Shirley, who was born in Paris. During the war they went to live in the South of France, which at that time was under Vichy control. I have always been close to this cousin, and we often visited each other once I had settled in London.

As I wanted to enjoy my time in London, I thought I should make contact with Tony. We went out on several occasions and seemed to get on well. When my mother and I flew over to Paris, I mentioned that I would be away for a few days, and Tony asked if he could join us for the weekend. This trip to Paris marks the beginning of our relationship.

After a brief courtship, we married in August 1951 and moved into a three bedroom apartment in St. Petersburg Place, just off Bayswater Road. It was very difficult to find appropriate housing at that time, as there had been extensive bombing in all areas of the city. The housing shortage was still a major issue of the time. Between 1945 and 1948, more than 156,000 prefabricated homes were built to help ease this shortage. These were mainly bungalows, of which many exceeded their expected lifespan and survived well into the 1960s and later.

Around this time I remember jokingly making a comment to Ruth that if the marriage didn't work out I could always get a divorce. Of course, this was highly frowned upon then, but was still a genuine possibility.

Tony was charming, sophisticated, loved going out and had a very large social circle. He was an overly generous person, quite often to the extent that he would embarrass his friends and associates by always insisting on paying the check. This generosity was also afforded to me. If I asked him for one handbag, he would buy me two.

Marrying Tony introduced me to a new, exciting way of living. During this time, I enjoyed a privileged lifestyle and was altogether spoilt. I was able to lie in bed mid-morning, and spent my days shopping and meeting my friends for lunch or afternoon tea. I even had a woman, Mrs Grimes, who came every day to clean the apartment. Part of her job included bringing me tea and coffee in bed with toast.

Above all, Tony introduced me to the London of the 1950s, and it was an electrifying experience for a young woman. Even though it was a time of austerity, we wouldn't have known it.

Our evenings were spent with a dinner out, a visit to the theatre or a West End musical, of which there were many on offer as it was the golden age of musicals. To name just a few, we saw classics like *Oklahoma, Guys and Dolls* and *South Pacific.* We also went to the London Palladium on a regular basis, and I was fortunate enough to see the great stars of variety of that Era including Judy Garland, Danny Kay, and many other variety personalities. Whatever entertainment we chose for the evening, we would invariably end up at one of the more popular night clubs of the time, dancing until the early hours.

It was at the Stork club on Argyle Street that I first saw Elizabeth Taylor. She was dancing with her then husband, Michael Wilding. I saw her one other time, a few years later at Royal Ascot. By then she had married Michael Todd, the supposed love of her life, who tragically died in an air crash not long after I saw them together.

Whilst shopping on Bond Street, I saw Ava Gardener, probably the most beautiful woman I had ever seen. I can assure you that she was even more striking in real life than on screen. I approached her and, like a star struck little girl, told her how I had always admired her performances in the movies she had been in.

We spent our summer holidays in the South of France either at Cannes or Juan Les Pins, as did our large circle of friends. These holidays involved lots of sunbathing and swimming during the day. The evenings were spent at the casino in Monte Carlo. During the winter we went skiing in Zermatt, Switzerland, or Val D'Isere, France. Tony would often be away on business in France or Italy. Sometimes I would accompany him.

Like many young girls of my generation, I went into my first marriage as a way to leave home and escape parental control. I didn't marry for love; I married for freedom. I have to admit that I was enticed by the extravagant lifestyle that I knew would come with marrying Tony.

The pairing seemed to suit everyone. Of course, my parents approved of the match. It also suited me as I could be his arm candy. It allowed me to experience this rather indulgent level of affluence. At the time, nothing could have made me happier. Looking back at this now, this lack of sentiment makes me shudder. I am aware of how shallow my perception was of what constituted the good life. But, at that time, this was all that mattered to me. Now that I have matured and I can look back with hindsight, I like to think that perhaps I needed to live this way to get it out of my system. By living like this, I was able to overcome this kind of superficiality and eventually evolve into the person I am today.

THE DRIVER

At the time that I married, it was very rare for a woman to learn how to drive. I found myself with a lot of time on my hands and thought that it would be a useful skill to acquire. So I began to take driving lessons, which cost just £1 per lesson. London was a fantastic city to learn to drive in. Even though the traffic was nowhere near as congested as what we see today, it was still a lot more demanding than learning in the countryside.

I passed my test first time around. I will never be sure whether this was due to my excellent handling of the car or whether the examiner's mind was swayed by the pair of stockings I chose to wear that day. They were very fashionable and had an intricate design from the heel to the ankle with a seam running up the middle of the calf. I noticed that he was admiring them, and, when he realised he had been caught out, let me know that they were fetching. In the end, I passed the test despite reversing onto the pavement whilst performing a three-point turn.

I had recently come into some money of my own and decided to use it to purchase my first car. At the end of the war, Germany was made to pay reparations for the atrocities committed. My father received a large sum of money as a means of redressing our family's suffering and loss. My father divided the compensation amongst the family; I put my share towards the car. It was a rather eye-catching green and white convertible Austin Metropolitan. Only a limited number were made, because eventually they were deemed unsafe, as the wheel base was too narrow and the car was prone to skidding. Unfortunately, I never took a photograph of the original, but once saw a red and white hardtop version of the exact same model on a visit to a car museum. I promptly snapped it up and keep a photograph of that as a memento instead.

I had attempted, if rather briefly, to learn to drive once before whilst I was in America. Herman had a car and had tried to teach me. He was unsuccessful. To this day I remember how awful this experience was. He sat me in the driver's seat, got in the back and, after a short instructional speech, simply ordered me to drive. Of course, I was useless. He just sat at the back criticising me, shouting commands and instructions that didn't help at all.

MARRIED LIFE

Tony liked to keep an open house, as this was how his family had lived in Lithuania, prior to the Nazi occupation. Any friends who felt like popping in were more than welcome to do so. They just turned up when they wanted, in and out, for meals and drinks. Sometimes as late as eleven o'clock in the evening, someone would suggest that we go out to a night club, and off we all went.

Tony and I were celebrated for our parties. As the hostess, this was something I took a lot of pride in. Because we had such a large group of friends, our parties were always a lot of fun. Our flat was reasonably big with three bedrooms, but we did our best to fit in as many people as possible. It was quite often the case that we had squeezed so many of our friends in that we couldn't physically let another person in. We were all packed in together so close and intimate that everyone got to know each other really well. This led to an unusually social, friendly atmosphere. Some of our guests, perhaps, got to know each other too well! What can I say? It was the Fifties. Everyone was young, happy and felt a compulsion to enjoy their post-war freedom. Due to my inherent disposition to act the good-girl, I was always proper and well-behaved. Of course, we had to invite the neighbours so they wouldn't complain.

The consequence of this was that Tony and I were very rarely alone. As a young wife, I felt that we needed more time together. The situation reawakened some of the vulnerabilities I had suffered from when I was young. As a child, being the youngest, I often found myself alone. If I was taken along with my brothers and sisters, they would have to constantly keep an eye on me and I could tell that they resented this. I was nothing but a nuisance for them. As much as I dislike admitting it, deep down, I wanted to be the centre of attention, both with my siblings and my new husband. What I wanted was to be made a fuss of. To me this was my husband's job; it was his duty as a loving spouse.

Tony's business demanded that he worked long hours every single day. As well as owning an import/export jewellery business, he also dabbled in another company managed by his cousin that dealt in war surplus items. I couldn't help but feel that there was too much space between us, whether it was because Tony was working late, was away in another country on business or because we were always surrounded by other people. Even on our first few dates, he took me out as part of a group. There wasn't enough intimacy to build up the closeness that I had expected. I think this was the main reason that I wasn't content with the relationship.

I always had Ruth and continued to spend a lot of time with her. I also became good friends with many of Tony's large group of acquaintances. Lots of his friends were bachelors, some of whom would live with girlfriends with no intention of ever getting married. This was still relatively uncommon at the time. A lot these men insisted on the benefits of a "solitary" life, although they were never really alone. They were always playing the field and kept the company of a lot of different girls, quite often at the same time. There were quite a lot of freeloaders in this crowd too, but, of course, Tony was more than happy to pay for their share of the fun.

At that time all my friends were continental, by which I mean that none of them had been born in Britain, most having arrived at different stages during the 1930s. They were from Hungary, Czechoslovakia, Austria, France, Germany, Lithuania, Poland, and there were others who were survivors of the concentration camps. What I found so amazing is how normal and joyous they were after all the trauma they had experienced. During the next few years, I came across many survivors of the concentration camps and found that they all had a wonderful spirit and zest for life, as if they needed to live for all the others who had not survived.

There was a café just behind Selfridges that was a very popular meeting place for us, called The Wayfarer. This café-restaurant was always jam-packed with Europeans, and the sound of violins and accordions were constantly playing in the different parts of the establishment. London had adopted a continental culture and had become a café society. The first coffee shops began to appear in the middle of the 1950s. I believe the first one was located in Park Lane, close to the Grosvenor Hotel. The other places that were popular were the lobbies of the Regent and Cumberland hotels.

A BABY BOY

In April 1953, Tony and I had a son, Paul, born by caesarean section at the Welbeck Street Clinic. I had a maternity nurse to accompany me back home after a two-week stay at the clinic. She stayed for a further four weeks, and then I employed a Scottish nanny to take care of Paul. Her name was June and she was the loveliest young girl. I am still in touch with her to the present day. June stayed with us for two and a half years, but then immigrated to Australia and subsequently married there. I really missed her and so, as my son was getting close to three years old, we decided to employ a series of au pairs; some of whom were better than others. During the school holidays, my friends and I used to take our children all of various ages, to a holiday camp in Littlehampton near Bognor, and our husbands came to join us on the weekend.

BACK TO WORK

After a while, I began to become restless with such an easy-going lifestyle. It had just so happened that Tony had invested in a hairdressing salon off Bond Street. He suggested that I might like to manage the salon for a while to see whether that type of occupation suited me. I tried this out for several months but didn't find the work challenging enough, so he took on a manager to run the premises.

As Tony had an import/export business, he suggested that he could open an office on Berwick Street, which was the district for wholesale jewellers, selling fashion jewellery to the retail trade. This suggestion was more appealing to me as I was familiar with the trade. The only real difference was that my father's business had been focused on precious metals and diamonds. We decided to call the business Margot's Fashion Jewellery.

I felt that this was a way to prove myself as a business woman, capable of organising a successful business. I had one assistant manager, who saw to the company's affairs when I was not available, and sometimes Ruth came along for a few hours to assist. As well as procuring items directly from my husband's import business, I made an effort to seek out trade fairs to select merchandise particularly for my sort of customers. I could tell that this extra effort was worth it due to the repeat business I received from many of my customers, who always seemed to be highly appreciative of the product on offer at Margot's.

DIVORCE

Now that I was back to leading an active lifestyle, Tony and I began to drift even further apart. He continued to travel a great deal and worked ridiculously long hours. Other than socially, we really didn't spend much time together. Feeling a little disillusioned with my situation, I went to see my parents in Los Angeles to think things over.

I began to feel that this wasn't a healthy way to live. Having been brought up with a conventional family background and seeing how Ruth lived only accentuated this notion of mine. She had two young daughters and lived in a very nice house on Finchley Road. As she and I had always been extremely close, I confided in her about my concerns. My brother was also aware that I wasn't content with my marriage. Without going into details, Tony and I eventually agreed that the relationship wasn't viable and we divorced in 1959.

My family were supportive of my decision. This even included my father, who was initially quite upset with me. I think that, regardless of how disappointed they were, they soon began to sympathise because they knew that it was the right thing for me to do. What mattered most was that I knew it was the right thing for me to do. Ruth was very understanding and helpful. I moved into her flat immediately after the divorce and lived with her for six months.

With the benefit of hindsight I think that the main problem was that I was simply too young and immature for Tony, and perhaps he was more suited to life as a bachelor.

I have learnt since working as a therapist, with both couples and individuals, that divorce is never an easy option. If I compare our experience with that of the majority of couples that I have worked with, our divorce stands out as an amicable one. He remarried, and I really liked the woman he chose. She adored my son and was so well matched to Tony.

A NEW START

I continued to run the office for a little while and in due course met my present husband, Henry, who was one of my customers. The initial attraction we felt for each other was purely based on chemistry. He was an extremely good looking man and a very good listener. I felt that he was exactly the sort of man that would help me settle down and create the lifestyle that I needed to finally set down some roots.

I had also met his mother and father, as they occasionally joined him on his trips to my shop. His mother also ran a small jewellery shop in an arcade in Reading and enjoyed buying goods from me for her business. He lived in Reading, his family having moved there from the East End of London at the beginning of the war. Eventually, after seeing each other for some time, we decided to get married.

The lifestyle of my seven years of marriage to Tony had been exciting and fun; however, it was a restless, somewhat manic way of living.

The next part of this story covers the next fifty years of my life. I spent it all with Henry. Fifty years is a long, long time. As Henry, who has a great sense of humour, has often said when people comment on the length of our marriage, "Margot and I have only ever had one argument… and it still continues to this day!" or, the other comment, "You get twenty five years for murder! What have we done to serve two life sentences?"

CHAPTER FIVE 1960-1970

SWINGING SIXTIES

The changes that were happening in society around the whole world would have a great influence on how my generation began to look at life. There were major changes in society, most notably the civil rights movement and the advent of the sexual revolution. Society began to take a good hard look at itself. This had an effect on everybody, as the philosophies that were the engine of these movements eventually seeped into popular culture. This was largely down to the fact that most families now had a television in their front rooms.

Towards the end of the 1960s, there was instant news being shown on TV in full colour. We watched the moon landing on our televisions in the comfort of our front rooms. The whole world had front row seats to the aftermath of the assassination of an American president. The convenience and accessibility of this was actually quite an overwhelming experience for those of us who were used to acquiring knowledge of current affairs by listening to the radio and reading the newspaper. We were used to seeing newsreels at the cinema, but this was usually only a once-a-week occurrence.

On a more personal note, my generation, especially those from continental Europe and those with a Jewish heritage, were finally getting to grips with the freedom that we had found ourselves experiencing. Following the war years, we had not only been grateful to survive but were living with a sense of accomplishment of how we had managed our day-to-day existence. From the 1960s onward there was a shift toward thinking about the importance of personal freedom and the individual. This was something which paralleled my own experiences. All of sudden, we found ourselves with choices in food, shopping and travel.

In the 1950s, women had been enchanted with the NEW Look with tiny waists and calf-length skirts. Now miniskirts were all the rage, as were sculptured haircuts. Gone were the days of crimpy hair and harsh colours, now the look was sleek and sophisticated. The furniture of the time was G-plan and the colour was coffee and cream. Wallpapers were heavily textured and made of straw for that designer look.

All the while, the weird and wonderful world of the avant-garde was becoming more of an influence on popular culture. We started listening to music that at first sounded really quite strange, but soon delighted us. It was the Sixties.

HENRY

As I entered my thirties, I had as of yet been unable to gain any lasting stability in my life. I would like to think through little fault of my own. It was almost as if every time I blinked I found myself in a completely new situation, with strange surroundings for me to adapt to. One moment it was Germany, the next England. One day I was relaxing in sunny California, the next I was battling off the dogged wind and freezing rain of London. Of course, I had become accustomed to this kind of living. It was simply the way my life had panned out. I was now exceedingly proficient in adapting to change and making the most of any new environment. In many ways, it had been an exciting way to live that no doubt played an essential role in carving me into the person I am today; however, at that time, I had come to feel another change in me. This time I wanted to settle down. It just so happened that around this same time I met Henry.

I felt that Henry was exactly the sort of man that would help me settle down and create the lifestyle that I needed to finally lay down some roots. Both sides of his family had been settled in England for hundreds of years. On his mother's side, his ancestors had taken the opportunity to relocate to England when Cromwell had allowed the Jews to return in the seventeenth century. While Cromwell never authorized any invitation or readmission of Jews to Britain, a small colony of Sephardic Jews, who had original come from Portugal and Spain to escape the Spanish Inquisition, were identified in 1656 and allowed to remain living in London. Henry's mothers' maiden name was Garcia. She came from a very large East London family, who now mainly dealt in the fruit business and ran market stalls at Petticoat Lane.

His father's family was of Dutch descent. The Dutch Jews who arrived in London were often referred to as Chuts and more often than not came from Amsterdam. They had brought with them an expertise in a number of trades, particularly cigar making; although, Henry's great grandfather and grandfather were both fishmongers.

Henry's parents and close family were very different from the people that I had been used to mixing with. As my family had originated from Poland and lived in Germany, I was used to a more continental style of living. All my life I had been surrounded by a variety of people from many European countries. Even in London during the 1950s, the company I kept was primarily continental. It took me a while to adapt to this new kind of family environment. Even the food was somewhat different to that which I had been accustomed.

His parents both came from large families. Mick had six brothers and two sisters; Rosie had four brothers and two sisters.

Henrys' brother Roy, who suffered from Down's syndrome, was six years younger than Henry and was a greatly adored member of his family. He was relatively independent and initially attended a special school before subsequently frequenting a work center. He was able to go to the work center by himself, taking two buses for the journey. He attended all the family celebrations and often went on holiday with his parents. Their favorite holiday location was Majorca.

I have included all this about Henry's family not just for exposition, but because I think it is important. The stability of Henry's background was a foundation for me to find my own.

Meanwhile, I had been living with Ruth and her family after the breakup of my first marriage. Following my decision to remarry, it seemed sensible to move closer to where Henry lived, so that I could get to know the area better. So in 1960 I moved to Reading. Henry was extremely close to his family, still living at home with them at the age of twenty-nine and, in fact, continued to do so until we married in 1961.

I rented a house in Earley, moving there with Paul, who was then aged six. The house in Earley was a semi-detached property probably built in the 1920s. It had three bedrooms, a small kitchen, dining room and lounge. It was furnished and suitable for the purpose, until Henry and I found a house that we could settle in. I lived there for a whole year.

Paul initially started at a prep school and spent his weekdays with me. Every weekend he was picked up from Reading Station by the au pair, who had continued to work for Tony. Two years later, at the age of eight, he began as a boarder at Carmel College, a Jewish public school in Wallingford. Because his father had attended boarding school, it had always been understood that Paul would do the same. In retrospect, I believe eight years old is far too young to send a child away from home to boarding school, but at the time I didn't realise this.

A DREAM HOME

Eventually, Henry and I bought a house in Sonning, a beautiful, quaint little village in Berkshire that has the river Thames flowing through it. The house itself was a dream house. It had been built in 1957 and had been used as a show house. It was even shown at the ideal home exhibition. In my mind, we were very much moving into the ideal home. It was very beautiful for that day and age and made an instant impression on us. We fell in love with it, so much so that we remained living there for half a century.

When we bought the house and showed it to Henry's parents, my father-in-law agreed that it was a beautiful house but couldn't understand why anyone would choose to live in the country. The house was exactly three miles from the centre of Reading, where they were living at that time. Not exactly the middle of nowhere. Personally, I thought it was a great location.

It was the biggest house I had ever lived in and was just for me and Henry. The accommodation consisted of four bedrooms, a lounge, dining room, kitchen and a large garden. What excited me most was the opportunity to make my own mark on a property that was entirely mine, a property which I personally owned. Of course, I only owned half of it, as Henry and I had bought it in joint names. Needless to say, I got stuck in straight away decorating and furnishing the rooms and working in the garden. It was the first time I had personally put down roots; so I wanted to make the most of this unique opportunity in every single way that I could.

Although the kitchen was modern for the times in this country, it wasn't up to the standard of the American kitchens I had known and grown accustomed to in California. I immediately started to make changes. Our friends thought I had gone mad. So many of them pleaded with me not to change a thing, asking me why on earth would I want to ruin such a lovely kitchen. I paid no attention to them. I imagine Henry thought the same, but by then he knew me well and didn't attempt to discourage me. He had learnt to trust my judgment. The first thing I did was to install a Moffat stainless steel wall-oven.

I decorated the bedroom walls with white, black and gold Regency stripe wallpaper, and the ceiling in a wallpaper design of golden stars. The black and turquoise bathroom, completely tiled from floor to ceiling, was also quite typical and stylish for that era. The only change was that the floor was tiled with Amtico tiles that were of such excellent quality that when we sold the house nearly fifty years later they were still in as fine a condition as they were when they were first installed.

The garden was enormous, a third of an acre in size. I couldn't wait to rekindle my love of gardening and get my hands dirty, utilising all the gardening skills I had learnt as a young girl. I had previously been in charge of a small plot of land in our garden in Crouch End during the 1940s. That little plot of land was positively miniscule in comparison to the huge, blank canvas that I was now presented with. The garden was so big and the original layout so uninteresting that I thought it necessary to employ some landscape gardeners to help me with my project. They installed a lovely rockery and planted a wide variety of different species of tree. I picked out a selection of shrubs, potted plants and hanging baskets, and also kept a vegetable patch, in homage to the cute, little one I had enjoyed caring over so many years before.

LONDON

Initially, I missed living in London. In particular, I missed being able to pop over to see Ruth whenever I felt like it. To deal with this I set aside the time to journey into London twice a week to meet her, normally in Selfridges for coffee and some shopping. From Reading Station it only took thirty-five minutes for the train to arrive at London Paddington, and the fare for a return ticket cost only five shillings.

The trains back then were steam locomotives. On a windy day, if the windows were left open, pieces of smut would lightly cascade into the carriages like dirty snowflakes and settle on your clothing. The steam locomotives gradually evolved into diesel trains. Train travel has changed a lot over the years, most noticeably in price. In the present day, an off-peak day return travel card costs a little over £16. The difference is tremendous. A casual outing to London has become an expensive trip. Back then, there was no financial worry in jumping on the train.

We would also frequently drive up to London on the weekend for lunch or dinner. We were always welcome at Ruth's. She just loved to entertain and was such a fantastic cook.

I also used these daytrips into London to get ideas and inspiration for furnishing our new home, which involved frequenting places like Kensington High Street for the Biba store, Tottenham Court Road for Heals and Habitat and Carnaby Street for its extensive variety of fashionable boutiques. At that time, there were no shopping malls or out of town shopping centres. Everybody would have to make the journey to Central London, to Oxford St., Regent

St., Bond St., Knightsbridge or Kensington High St, to do their shopping. Also, outside London, most town centres would have half-day closing either on Wednesday or Thursday and often a half day on Saturday.

There was no Sunday shopping, except for Petticoat Lane in the East End of London, which had been given permission to trade because it didn't open for Saturday trading. This was because, when the licence was originally granted, there was a very large Jewish population in the East End of London that observed the Sabbath. Because everything else was closed on a Sunday, the general public flocked to Petticoat Lane and it became established as a tourist attraction. Coaches full of visitors would arrive from all over the country, as people visiting London would include Petticoat Lane as part of their sightseeing tours.

During the 1980s, Henry and I took the opportunity to run one of the stalls there, as one had become available. It was notoriously difficult to acquire one of these stalls, as they were passed down through families. Once a family had been awarded a licence, they were permitted to pass them on to members of their family but were never allowed to sell it. So, when there was no one else to take the family's allocation, to avoid losing the stall forever, we took control of it. I will mention more about this in due course.

MARRIAGE

Henry and I were married in July, 1961. I really wasn't keen on a large wedding but, as Henry was the only son who would be married, I agreed to go along with a ceremony in the New Synagogue in London, just off Edgware Road. We held the reception at Skindles Hotel in Maidenhead. Skindles was a very popular riverside hotel. Henry was very friendly with the owner, having spent many years going there for drinks and dinner. The setting by the Maidenhead Bridge with tables on the lawns was just perfect; plus it was a beautiful, sunny day. Ruth and Jack attended with their families. My parents were living in California and felt it was too much trouble to attend, as they didn't have British citizenship and hadn't yet acquired their American passports. This was a shame, but it couldn't be avoided.

The whole day, the wedding and the reception, was thoroughly enjoyable. Something happened at the reception that still makes me laugh, involving the chauffeurs that had come from London. When they arrived at Skindles, we were standing in line at the reception, which was near the bar. As they were dressed formally, they were mistaken for guests and offered drinks. For whatever reason, and with a complete disregard for professionalism, they decided to involve themselves in the reception. At one point, Henry turned to me and asked me who these men were and how they were related to my family. I responded by asking him exactly the same question.

During fifty years of marriage, a couple will undergo countless changes as a relationship can't help but continually develop. These changes will be complimentary as well as restricting. Learning to cope with this healthy mix of covenant and conflict ensures the growth of both individuals and leads to a more satisfactory union. Personally, I feel like the key to marriage is balancing one's desire to share one's life with someone and one's need to remain autonomous. This is something Henry and I still sometimes struggle with today, but over the years we have become adept at dealing with our troubles when and if they arrive. After fifty-one years of marriage we are… still here!

There has been a lot of compromise and adaption, as there needs to be in any relationship in order to make it function. In his book, *The Road Less Travelled*, M Scott Peck, an eminent psychologist, offers a description of marriage which mirrors the way in which I have grown to think of it. Since it precisely parallels my thoughts, I feel it merits inclusion. Furthermore, I don't think I could add much more to Peck's astute and accurate insight.

"As I have grown… I have come to realise that it is the separateness of the partners that enriches the union. Great marriages cannot be constructed by individuals that are terrified by their basic aloneness as so commonly is the case, and seek a merging in marriage. Genuine love not only respects the individuality of the other, but actually seeks to cultivate it, even at the risk of separation or loss. The ultimate goal of life remains the spiritual growth of the individual, the solitary journey to peaks that can only be climbed alone. Significant journeys cannot be accomplished without the nurture provided by a successful marriage. But as is the case with all genuine love, "Sacrifices" on behalf of growth of the other result in equal or greater growth of the self." – M Scott Peck

BETTING SHOP

We decided against going on a honeymoon at that time, as my father-in-law, Mickey, had recently opened a betting shop, the first betting shop in Reading. Betting shops had recently been legalized by Harold Macmillan's Conservative government. Mickey had been an on-course bookmaker for many years when the only gambling allowed in England was at race tracks. He would attend all the major meetings across the country including Ascot, Goodwood, Newbury and Cheltenham.

Henry had never been interested in the racing business; nevertheless, he would often clerk for his father in the evenings, as Mickey had a stand at the Reading Greyhound Stadium. His job was to take the bets. Henry told me that he never took any pleasure from this task and only offered to do it in order to help his father.

Once I had settled into our new home, Mickey asked me whether I would be interested in a part-time role working with him in the betting shop. I knew absolutely nothing about the racing business, but he said that it wouldn't take me long to pick up the basics. It sounded quite interesting, and, as I was always up for a challenge, I agreed to give it a try. I couldn't think of any reason not to. My only initial reservation was that I was needed to pick up my son from school, but this wasn't a problem. The working hours fitted in perfectly with the school run. This was before my son was sent off to boarding school.

My job was to take our customers' bets during the lunch hour and then enter the transactions into the ledger. I had to learn all the different types of bet that could be placed on the wide variety of selections. For example, there was "Win only", "Each way", "Double", "Treble" and "Yankee Bet". The last of these, the Yankee Bet, was the most complex, and, if my memory serves me well, involved choosing six doubles, four trebles and one accumulator from four selected horses, eleven selections in all. Sometimes the punters were very lucky and scooped the lot.

I read *Sporting Life* each day to gain some insight into which horses were being entered in the various races at the major racecourses. I also made an effort to find out which horses and jockeys were in winning form, even though it wasn't necessary to know this kind of information; I just liked being in the know. Compared to today's luxury betting establishments, the shops at that time were very basic. There was no seating, no television, no electronic timers, no scanners or any security measures. Only racing commentary was permitted.

The busiest days were the Grand National and Derby Day. We took thousands of bets with each one having to be settled and checked by hand, as this was before computerized technology. We were always highly amused when the winning ticket holders rushed in expecting an immediate payout as soon as the race had finished. Processing the bets was an extremely tedious task, and our amusement soon turned to irritation whenever we were made to hurry.

Our clientele varied from Irish builders to office workers to shop staff from John Lewis and other stores. As well as this, a number of friendly police officers would pop by for a cup of tea and to place a bet. They were always very pleasant and would invariably turn a blind eye to the fact that I 'illegally' parked my car outside the shop each day. Though I must say, back then, the traffic on Minster Street and other areas of Reading was minimal. There was one regular that worked as the chef at a local hotel. He has stuck in my memory because, whenever he came into the shop and for however long he stayed, he would constantly be picking his nose. I knew which hotel he worked in and made a point of never going there to eat. After a while, I became so familiar with the clientele that I was able to recognize and link the handwritten slips and type of bet placed to the individual punters, even if I hadn't taken the bet.

The punters could get quite noisy and their behaviour would often border on becoming a problem. The pubs would close at two o'clock in the afternoon, as those were the days before extended opening hours, and our clientele would regularly saunter in a little worse for wear to see if their bets had come in. It was also a highly competitive environment, where the mood of our punters could abruptly sway between the vicissitudes of ecstasy and despair, depending on whether lady luck was with them or not.

We never had any serious problems, nothing I couldn't handle. The punters were only ever tipsy, never blind drunk. Mickey made it my job to ensure that things never got out of hand. It always amused me that these rowdy, mainly working class men would always listen to me. I was only small and there was only one of me. The truth is that, in general, men were a lot more respectful to woman back then. All I had to do was push the right buttons and they would calm down. A quick threat that I wouldn't take any more bets and their boisterous behaviour would die down instantly.

HONEYMOON

As we didn't have a honeymoon, we decided to go away the following year for a Caribbean cruise. At that time, the French Line laid on three four-week cruises around the Caribbean on their usual banana run. The ships used were the *Antilles* and the *Flandres*.

We couldn't decide whether to go during February or March. I suggested March as my niece Terry was getting married at the beginning of April, and we both wanted to look suntanned. Again, this recurring desire for a suntan! In those days the phenomenon of package holidays and cruises hadn't yet become the established holiday choice that they are today. For most people, a winter cruise was seen as a great luxury. For £250 each, we booked the cruise for March 1962. As we had booked it well in advance, in July, I spent the next few months making beautiful evening gowns, as we had booked to go first class and evening wear was mandatory. Henry purchased a rather elegant white dinner jacket for the holiday.

As March approached and the day of our voyage grew ever closer, our excitement increased immeasurably.

We had decided to go to Southampton on the day before the *Antilles* was to sail from Le Havre. On the day of our departure, we awoke to particularly bad weather for that time of year. The weather was cold and rather dismal. It had been snowing overnight, so the streets were now covered in sleet and slush. It was the perfect weather to escape from. We sat down for our breakfast. The boat wasn't due until around ten o'clock in the morning. We ordered our taxi to take us to the docks for midday. I insisted on taking a seasick tablet, as I dreaded the thought of being seasick.

At about eleven o'clock, the hotel manager informed us that our cruise ship had been delayed in Le Havre, but that it should arrive early in the afternoon. He offered us lunch for the inconvenience caused. Soon after we had eaten our lunch, Henry became restless and wandered down to the docks. I sat on my own looking out at the ocean, dreaming about the clear waters and the glorious sunshine I would soon be surrounded by. I couldn't wait to get away from this awful weather. When Henry returned, the manager once again came over to us. He looked incredibly sheepish, as this time he was bearing even more unfortunate news. He told us that the crew had gone on strike and that the French Line had cancelled our cruise.

The disappointment was terrible; the frustration unbearable. We were so disheartened that we even began to get angry at ourselves, as we found out later that out of three possible sailings the one we had chosen was the only one to be cancelled. I told Henry that I was ashamed to go home and that he had to find us another place to go. To think that all the dresses I had made would go to waste!

We returned home and unpacked. When we called Henry's parents and then Ruth, they thought we were joking. If only! The next day we went up to the head office of Thomas Cook in Berkeley Square, where we had booked the cruise originally, and told them that they had to find us another holiday with guaranteed sunshine. They suggested the Canary Islands. We were able to get a flight out there quite quickly and ended up having a very pleasant two-week holiday, although we never quite overcame the shock of that cancelled cruise. Even in the present, we rarely book a holiday more than six to eight weeks in advance.

PLANE TRAVEL

During the Early Sixties, the world was far less paranoid than it is today. Everybody felt a whole lot safer. It was a time of great security. There were a few conflicts in the world, but none that really affected the people of Britain.

On the weekend, we would frequently go to a restaurant at London Airport that had a balcony overlooking the Apron, where the long distance planes taxied right up to the entrance of the custom halls for the passengers to disembark directly into the airport. We were more than happy to pass a couple of hours enjoying tea and cakes, people watching. It was a really pleasant, relaxing environment. The kind of place you could easily spend a fun day out with the family. We used to take Paul to the viewing tower to take photos of the different planes landing and taking off on the runway. I recall that during the 1950s when I visited Paris to see Shirley or Aunt Fanny, I usually took what was called the Champagne flight in the middle of the day. At that time it was not unusual for the Captain to walk through the cabin, and inquire how the passengers were enjoying their flight. The Captain would also leave the cockpit door open, and tell the passengers what sort of weather to expect. On one of my return journeys from Paris, after speaking to some other passengers, the Captain approached me and asked whether I would be interested to sit in the cockpit and watch as the plane landed at Heathrow. How could I refuse such an offer! How times have changed. In the present, I find it really hard to get used to the heightened security we see at airports, especially the armed guards patrolling the check-in areas.

The first time I encountered this kind of heightened security was in 1978, when I went to visit Paul in Israel. I flew on the Israeli Air line, EL AL. The check-in procedures were very stringent, and there were armed security police everywhere you looked. These measures were implemented on account of the massacre of the members of the Israeli team during the Summer Olympics of 1972 in Munich.

A MAN'S WORLD

Now that Paul was at boarding school, I found myself with large amounts of free time. I decided that I wanted to further my knowledge and began to attend courses at Woodley Hill House, which was part of Bracknell College, and the Reading Polytechnic College. Initially it was the homemaker subjects, such as freezer cookery, yeast baking and flower arranging, that were more to my interest. Then I signed on for dressmaking, pottery, art and knitting. The course in knitting was particularly useful, as it taught me to design coats and knitted suits, which were in vogue at the time.

After this, I thought learning Spanish might come in handy. I also attended a short course on the technique of rapid reading. The reason I took the rapid reading course was that Henry could read books at a rate of one a day. I loved to read and hated the fact that I could never keep up with him. The course taught me how to skim through pages and pages of print, all the while keeping up with the story and absorbing the intricacies of character and plot. I was the only woman in a class of twenty. This immediately awakened the female competitor in me. I had to make sure that I was reading quicker than the men. Because I put so much effort into achieving this, I quickly became tired of it and reverted back to my usual snail's pace, savouring the books and their stories.

At some point during the 1960s, I applied for a job as a sales representative. I enjoyed driving, and equally enjoyed selling, so would regularly look at the sales jobs that were available in the local papers.

I saw an advert in the Reading Chronicle for a sales representative of a company called Farley's Rusks that distributed baby rusks. The brief was to visit chemist shops to take orders and to top up on stock. I knew that I could do all of this easily, so I arranged an appointment to be interviewed at a hotel in Reading. At the interview, they told me that I had all the right skills for the job, but that, being a woman, I wasn't what they were looking for. Salespersons at that time were usually men. Women's liberation had not fully kicked off yet.

So the next thing I tried was a job performing in-store demonstrations for what were mainly wine and cheese companies. This was something I really enjoyed. I worked for an agency, who would contact me whenever they had work for me in the area. Sometimes we had to wear uniforms or costumes as part of the advertising campaign for the product. The reason I enjoyed this type of work was that there was such great variety in the products that I worked with. It was also very social, and I met lots of different people from all areas of Berkshire, Oxfordshire and Buckinghamshire.

LOSS

This period of time was marred by the tragic death of my lovely, little niece Lynette, who at the age of eleven died of liver cancer. Lynette was Jack and Jessie's youngest daughter. Our whole family was absolutely devastated, but I know that Jack and Jessie never really recovered from their loss. They both dealt with it in different ways and their marriage began to fall apart. Eventually, they divorced, and Jack remarried. Jessie unfortunately experienced periodic depressions. She was very close to her eldest daughter, Terry, who is just twelve years younger than me, and together they helped each other through these tough times.

I remember how proud I was when I became an aunty at the age of twelve. At that time they only lived a five minutes' walk away from where we lived, and I frequently went around to their house to take Terry for walks and play with her.

PARENTS' RETURN

In 1965, my parents, in particular my father, decided to return to live in London. He had retired and sold half of his business; Herman took over the rest. My mother had not been too well and was slowing down. He thought that it would be better for them to be close to their daughters as they grew older. Ruth's home had been converted into two separate apartments when Paula had left for New Zealand. At the time, they were letting this flat. When Ruth heard that our parents were interested in returning to London, she offered them the opportunity to let it.

I don't think my mother was happy at my father's choice to return to London, as she enjoyed the warmth of the Los Angeles climate. To make matters worse, the journey to London took a lot out of her.

Both Henry and I thought it was a wonderful idea. In hindsight, having now reached old age myself, I feel that an upheaval of that kind at that stage of her life must have been unsettling for her. Her grandchildren were growing up and were busy, noisy and just getting on with their own lives, which meant that she really didn't see too much of them. I wouldn't be surprised if she didn't really want to be too involved with them. Having survived all the highs and lows of bringing five children into the world and doing so in what was at times such a difficult and hostile environment, she must have loved the peace and quiet of being able to take a step back and think solely about herself. I have recently become aware of how important it is to have some quality personal space once one has entered one's senior years.

They returned to the UK in 1965. For the first few years, my mother was still quite active. She was particularly delighted when her two sisters came to visit in 1966 and stayed at the Brent Bridge Hotel, the same time as the English football team that won the World Cup was staying there. It was the last time all three sisters were together.

THE LAUNDERETTE

Ruth and her husband had invested in a launderette business in London in the Late Fifties and found it to be a successful business venture. Their launderettes were situated on Kilburn High Road, which had a dense bedsit population, who all needed washing machine facilities. It was an ideal location for this type of business.

Looking for another means of income, we explored the launderette industry and decided to invest in it. We found premises located on Caversham Road, Reading, and invested five thousand pounds in the equipment and premises. We employed a manager to run the place.

Unfortunately, Reading wasn't London. It didn't have the density of population required to turn the launderette into a viable business. We kept it for three years, having to go in each day to check it out and mend the fuses on various machines. Fortunately, after three years, when we finally sold it, we were able to get our investment back. It was a huge relief. When Henry and I finally signed off on the handover of the business, we both said we felt like a great weight had been lifted. I felt like the genie in *Aladdin* who, on being released from his imprisonment inside the lamp, shouted out: "I am free!"

OUR DINNER PARTIES

Reflecting on my behaviour and lifestyle during the 1960s, I now recognise it as bearing the characteristics of the nesting phase. The roots had been put down. Now I felt the need to become a domestic goddess. I wanted to be seen as someone who ran her household with grace and efficiency and who was proficient in cooking, baking, making jam and all the various other bits and pieces that were expected of the dutiful wife during that era. I absolutely revelled in this role. The courses I took at Woodley Hill House certainly helped with this.

Throughout the decade, we held a string of dinner parties. This was a popular way to entertain during the 1960s and 1970s. At first our motivation was that we had moved into our new house and wanted to show it off, but Henry and I enjoyed hosting these events so much that we kept organising more. The key was to select the right guests so that the evening would be full of interesting conversation and never become dull or tiresome.

These dinner parties were quite formal events. I set out my best china and cutlery. The tables were dressed with beautiful tablecloths rather than place mats, which are now the current fashion. I completed the look with artistic flower arrangements that were usually based on Ikebana, the Japanese design, which I had learned from attending flower arranging courses. After the meal we offered a selection of cigarettes in an onyx cigarette box and matching table lighter. To bring the dinner to an end, we drank brandy and liqueurs, and passed around a box of After Eight chocolates.

I always kept a list of everyone that had come to a certain evening to ensure I didn't give them the same food two times running. I took it all quite seriously. I wanted my guests to leave thinking, "That was a good evening!" To be honest, I had had a lot of practise with my hectic party life in London during the 1950s.

I tried to make sure I invited guests who would get along with each other, so I organised my friends into groups of what I thought were like-minded people. For instance, one evening I invited Joe our GP, my gynaecologist and one friend who specialised in ENT. I remember thinking that we had all our options covered in case of a medical emergency.

HENRY'S CAREER MOVE

In 1968, Henry's father sold his betting shop. He decided he was ready to retire. The jewelry business at that time wasn't exactly flourishing, so Henry decided to try his hand in the insurance industry. He took up a position within a firm in the City of London, Abbey Life, and enjoyed the challenges of this type of work. The product that was being sold was not merchandise, but life cover and investment bonds. I was pleased that he had decided to try a different career, as his education had been affected by changing schools when his family moved to Reading. Despite winning a scholarship to a grammar school, his parents had said there was no use in starting, as they would be returning to London when the war was finished. Of course, they never returned to London, and Henry missed out on the opportunity of a grammar school education. I always felt that he should have been an accountant, as he is and always has been brilliant with figures.

So, when he joined Abbey Life in the city, he did extremely well and worked there for a number of years. Above all he enjoyed the novelty of these new challenges and made good connections.

At the beginning of the 1970s, Abbey Life was expanding and decided to open an office in Reading. They said that it would be better if Henry based himself there. After a while, he found that it simply wasn't as stimulating working in the Reading office as it had been in the City, so decided to return to the jewelry business.

During 1969, we went to the South of France on vacation to visit my cousin Shirley, who at that time lived in Avignon. She was married to a bank manager, and they had one son together. Prior to her marriage she worked at Dior in Paris, so whenever I visited Paris in the fifties, she always made sure that she would obtain permission for me to attend fashion shows whilst I was there. Her husband was an international bridge player and was of a standard that he played with Omar Sharif, the film Star who was also renowned for his bridge playing

I remember their garden was full of fig trees. For breakfast, which we had outside in the garden enjoying the morning sunshine, we would pick figs. As we had so much enjoyment from the figs in Shirley's garden, we decided to plant a tree outside our kitchen window, that became enormous, and we enjoyed the fruit for many years, as surprisingly it thrived in our temperate climate despite the odds. We spent a few days with them and then drove on towards Cannes, where we had rented an apartment in a turning behind the Carlton Hotel, just minutes from the beach. It was a most enjoyable holiday, and we made plans to return the following year; however, it wasn't to be.

CHAPTER SIX 1970-1980

THE SEVENTIES

The hippie culture, which started in the latter half of the 1960s, had begun to wane by the early 1970s and faded towards the middle part of the decade. It was very much associated with a heightened political sensibility, which most notably involved mass opposition to the Vietnam War and nuclear armament. During the 1960s, each year on Easter Weekend, the anti-nuclear disarmament march came right past our home on the A4 from London into Reading and on towards Aldermaston. Although this had stopped by the 1970s, a march was held in 1972 on the original route, although there were significantly less people. In its heyday there were thousands taking part in these marches.

Mainstream culture had now adopted much of the ideology espoused by the hippies. So, as the demonstrations lost momentum, the impact of the hippies was already clear for everyone to see, a legacy which still continues to this day. Popular music, television, film, literature and the arts have all been greatly influenced by what went on during this period of cultural history. In society today, healthy living, outdoor music festivals and even contemporary sexual mores can be said to have evolved from the ideologies and cultural diversities encouraged during the Sixties and Early Seventies.

The political and economic liberty of women was an issue which arose in the 1960s, but only really started to take shape in any meaningful way as the 1970s wore on, with the advent of severely overdue debate petitioned by a whole host of women's lib movements. There was a neighbour of ours, a very intelligent woman, possibly in her early thirties, who was immersed in the world of politics. Towards the end of the decade, she was elected as a member of the European Parliament. This kind of thing was simply unheard of five years before.

The trend started with the rise of a significant number of women as heads of state and heads of government across a number of countries around the world, many being the first women to hold these positions. Particularly well-documented, largely because of

Evita, the popular musical by Andrew Lloyd Weber, was Isabel Martinez Peron, the first female president of Argentina. In India there was Indira Ghandi; in Britain Margaret Thatcher became the first female Prime Minister of the United Kingdom in 1979.

I first heard Margaret Thatcher speak at a prize-giving day at Carmel College, when she was Minister of Education and Science during the Edward Heath government.

In global affairs, industrialized countries, except Japan, experienced an economic recession due to an oil crisis caused by oil embargoes by the Organization of Arab Petroleum Exporting Countries (OPEC). The economic landscape started to look bleak again and people were reminded of the war and post-war years, when there were austerity measures in place.

In Britain, the IRA had started their terrorist activities, but, having survived the various bomb threats during the war, I still felt confident that the places I arranged to go were no threat to me. Radical American groups existed as well, such as the Weather Men. There was also the Munich Massacre at the 1972 summer Olympics, where Palestinian Arab terrorists of the Black September terrorist organization kidnapped and murdered eleven Israeli athletes.

On a more positive note, it was during the 1970s that people began to take notice of the dangers of smoking due to a series of public health warnings. I always liked being seen as trendy so gave up smoking when its reputation took a downward turn, much to the benefit of my health.

THE MATINEE

It was March 1970, and Henry was still working in the insurance business in the City. During this time, he would often discuss investment opportunities with our dear friend Joe, who was also our GP. It just so happened that a bond was issued which Henry thought would work out well for Joe. Henry didn't feel comfortable taking the commission for himself, so instead suggested that we put the money towards a big night out in London for both couples. Joe and his wife, Georgette, loved the sound of this idea. We agreed on a date and decided to go to a popular restaurant named the White Elephant on Curzon Street. Henry and I enjoyed eating out with Joe and Georgette. We tried out new venues on a regular basis.

As Henry and I knew it was going to be a late night, we decided to have a little siesta, or something like that, so that we would feel rested and rejuvenated for the evening. The matinee had the desired effect, as I remember having a really enjoyable evening; the food, in particular was spectacular. Our decision to take a siesta that day brought about an unexpected outcome.

A few weeks later, Joe and Georgette joined us again at another lovely restaurant in Berkshire that was renowned for its cordon bleu cuisine. The restaurant was used to train young chefs, so it had a varied menu and served excellent food at inexpensive prices.

During this meal I turned to Joe for some medical advice, as I thought there was a possibility I was entering the menopause. I was thirty-nine years old and had missed a couple of periods. He told me it was a possibility and that he would do some tests if I came by the surgery sometime. A week later, when the tests came back, he telephoned me personally and, laughing, said: "Forget about the menopause, you're pregnant!"

THE EARTH MOTHER

When we first married, Henry and I had thought it would be nice to have a child, but, after nearly ten years had passed without, we had accepted that it probably wasn't to be. With our active lifestyle, it didn't really matter to us either way.

When we found out about the pregnancy, we were a little concerned about my age, because at that time it was generally thought that the older you were the more likely the chance of having a child born with Down's syndrome. Henry's brother Roy had been born when his mother was thirty-six years old, so we had our concerns. It was also still common practice to have children earlier rather than later, unlike today where many women defer from having children in their twenties or early thirties because of their careers.

I asked my gynecologist what the risks were and whether I could have an amniotic fluid test. He responded that taking that option would risk miscarriage. We conceded that this was meant to be, and I continued happily with the pregnancy.

I was very adamant that I wanted to have a cesarean section, much like I had had for my first son. My reasoning for this was that I didn't want to try going into delivery first and then having to find out after many hours of acute discomfort that I needed a C section after all. Since working as a psychotherapist, I have met a number of women who have experienced an extremely lengthy birthing process, often up to forty eight hours, before going into theatre for a C section or a forceps delivery. The emotional trauma has often deprived them of the joy of being there for their new baby. Fortunately, this was not the case for me. I had a wonderful pregnancy, no problems whatsoever, and gave birth via caesarean section to a healthy son in October 1970.

We decided to call our son Lee. He was a lively, somewhat difficult baby. He took advantage of his parents' naivety and quickly figured out how to wrap us around his tiny little finger. With my first son, Paul, the vast majority of work had been handled by the maternity nurse. She would tell me when I needed to feed him; the rest had already been taken care of. Then June, my lovely nanny, took over, and I only had to play with him, which was lovely as he was such a well-behaved, well-brought up and contented child. As a baby, Paul was very sociable and friendly, was always beaming in photos and, perhaps most admirably, slept like a log.

So, although I had skimmed cursorily through a few books by Dr. Spock, I was otherwise a complete novice when it came to looking after babies. There was no two ways about it: I was what am usually referred to as an "anxious mother". It is often said that anxious mothers make anxious children. How true this is. I was overly anxious to do everything right, to make sure Lee wasn't hurt or harmed in any conceivable way. The problem was that there were so many potential risks to conceive of and therefore so many precautions to take. We were both particularly anxious when he was asleep because we had read a lot about cot death.

If someone had provided our son with some harder guidelines it would have done him, and us, some good. He needed a little discipline. As it was, we were too easy on him. This meant that we didn't get much sleep. Being a bright child he soon recognized that if he cried a little, mum and dad would get worried and give him their complete attention, immediately picking him up and comforting him. Every night he would perform his famous repertoire, to which Henry and I had front row seats.

After three and a half years, we suddenly became aware that Lee was actually sleeping through the night. It was such a relief, but by then we had become so accustomed to having less than five hours sleep that even to this day we find it impossible to stay in bed later than six o'clock. This has its advantages, as every morning at seven o'clock we are at the health club enjoying our daily swim.

In the present, I have no idea whether our son has any problem sleeping these days, as he left home many years ago. Despite my sleep deprivation, I really enjoyed the role of "Earth Mother".

THE ME DECADE

Following on from the communal lifestyle of the 1960s, the 1970s were often referred to as the "Me Decade". It was a time of self-awareness and the development of the Self. This philosophy resonated strongly with me and my constant drive to be independent, to prove to myself that I could create a business or career without the support of my family, and so I continued to explore what was out there that would fulfill me and give meaning to my life. For me, it marked the beginning of a new approach to looking at life.

I was influenced by the books that I started reading, the self-help books written by feminists and others who had been influenced by the liberation of the 1960s, "flower power" and the rights of the individual. Much of this literature came from California, and I was fascinated by the changing views of both males and females who had been influenced by these new freedoms.

A lot was made out of the connection between these philosophies and the hippie drug culture. It is true that people began to experiment more freely with recreational drugs and recreational sex and that this stemmed from, perhaps even spawned from this same freedom of self; however, this philosophy of individualism transcended any particular style of living and could be applied to anybody, however they chose to live.

Personally, I was never interested in taking any drugs. Whilst living in Los Angeles, I had been offered marijuana on several occasions; however, I was never tempted to try something that I might unwillingly become dependent on. This didn't mean that I couldn't be inspired by the same philosophies that inspired the hippie culture. A lot of these new kinds of philosophy were clumped together under the umbrella term, "New Age thinking". Yoga was one such philosophy that was included in this. I started yoga classes as it had become quite popular. Initially, I went because of an old injury to my back that I had suffered learning to dive in Los Angeles. It had since caused me considerable discomfort. It had been suggested that yoga would enable me to strengthen my spine and free me from some of this pain.

The decision to attend these yoga classes was one of the best I have ever made in my life. I was fortunate to have an excellent tutor and soon joined the British Wheel of Yoga, attending many seminars. At one stage, I even considered training to become a fully-licensed yoga tutor myself, but by then I had become interested in psychology and had already taken my first steps toward becoming a psychotherapist.

I was taken by the philosophy of yoga as much as I was by the physical benefits of it. This is when I became aware of the mind-body connection and the importance of maintaining balance in one's life. The direct connection between the well-being of our body and the well-being of our mind figures frequently in current psychological theories, and a lot of the most recent research verifies what yoga philosophers have always been aware of. In my current practice as a psychotherapist, I integrate some of the skills and ideas learned during my yoga training and have seen positive outcomes for my clients. This includes promoting the benefit of physical exercise and breathing exercises to clear the mind. Such simple activities can really calm us down and help us to reach an awareness of ourselves in the present.

MY MOTHER

In the early part of the decade, my mother's condition severely deteriorated. As well as her Parkinson's disease, she had become senile. Eventually, in 1972, when it was difficult to care for her at home, my father placed her in a nursing home. He worked out a schedule of visiting times for all the family to observe; this included Ruth, Jack and me, as well himself. So once a week I would go up in the morning after taking Henry to the station, as he was commuting to London daily at that time. Then I would drive up to North London with my eighteen-month-old child. I would take his lunch along and, as we needed to help my mother with her lunch, we would all eat together.

The whole experience wasn't pleasant for any of us. We would sit with her, but by that time she was not aware of the present and tended to live in another dimension, somewhere far away alone with her memories. Her sister, my Aunt Fanny, who had moved to London several years back and now lived near the nursing home, couldn't bring herself to visit, as she said it upset her too much seeing her sister like that. These visits made me feel desperately sad, as this poor old lady was not the mother I had known. The other thing that plagued me was that, if she was aware of how she looked, she would have hated to have been seen like that. This elegant woman, who had always cared so much about her appearance, was now a sad little old lady exposed to the harshest of life's inevitabilities.

In 1973, she caught pneumonia and passed away peacefully, aged seventy-six. I went to visit her the day before she died and was able to say goodbye to her. I was full of mixed emotions. The loss of one's beloved mother and first parent is always painful; however, for her sake as much as anything else, I was pleased that she was now at peace.

EXTENDING THE HOUSE

In 1972, Henry and I had considered moving to a larger house as we had been thinking about what would happen to his brother when his parents passed away. We came to a decision to extend the house, so that Roy could come to live with us when either his parents died or they became too old to care for him. So during the summer months of 1972, we lived in chaos whilst the back of the house was taken off and the house was doubled in size.

Two years later we had a swimming pool installed, as our youngest son had picked up infections when swimming in public pools that had caused him to be hospitalized with juvenile arthritis, known as Still's disease. Fortunately, the disease went into remission before causing any damage.

Early in 1973, I had a hysterectomy at the age of forty two, but made a very speedy recovery as I was fit had begun my yoga practice, and had also been reading about the benefits of vitamins and was taking a small selection such as Multi Vitamins and Fish oils. I am aware that many people do not believe in taking supplements, but I felt I would sooner have expensive urine, than deprive my body of something that would allow me to feel fit and energetic

EAR PIERCING

One day Ruth called me to say she had recently had her ears pierced in Selfridges. She told me that it was becoming fashionable again. There was a whole generation of woman who wouldn't have their ears pierced because they thought of it as common. Saying this, my mother had pierced ears, but she was a Victorian, having been born in 1897. I recall that she sometimes asked me to help her put her earrings in when her hands were becoming arthritic. I never felt particularly comfortable doing this.

Ruth described her experience as a non-event and told me that the ears were pierced with a type of staple gun that inserted the ear stud at the same time. When Henry next went to London on business, he made some enquiries and came back with this most peculiar of instruments. It really did look just like a staple gun and, in fact, functioned much in the same way as a staple gun, although instead of dealing in the perforation of paper it dealt with human flesh.

I suggested that I should get my ears pierced and experience the process because only then would I know whether I was comfortable performing the operation on others. I called in Joe and asked him to pierce one of my ears. I thought that having a GP there meant I would be in good hands if something were to go wrong. I let Henry pierce the other one. After a great deal of nervous apprehension, it turned out to be a non-event. So we discussed whether this could be something I could do in my spare time, as my son was now in nursery school, meaning that I had more spare time.

Joe had suggested I practice on some bacon rind, saying that it was the nearest texture to human skin. After practicing for a while and using some of my friends as guinea pigs, I felt confident enough to place an advert in the local paper, which read: "Ear Piercing by Appointment". I took out some insurance and equipped myself with a black briefcase and some surgical wipes. When visiting a client, I would carry a box of gold and silver earrings along with my ear piercing equipment.

The process was very simple. For most people it wasn't painful at all, but I found that earlobes vary in size. So for some there were some minor complications. This was especially the case with people who had particularly small earlobes. With these cases, I had to be careful not to infect the cartilage. After the piercing I swiftly disinfected the opening and then taught my client the appropriate ways of cleaning it.

I did this for several years. Sometimes I ended up having ear piercing parties, where a woman invited some of her friends to join her in having her ears pierced. Often a glass or two of wine was on offer to relax them for the procedure. The women who attended often wanted to buy different styles of earrings from me whilst I was there, so eventually I would bring along a selection of gold and silver chains, bracelets, brooches and earrings. I extended my customer base to include some of the workers from large IT companies in business parks around Berkshire and other areas within a thirty mile radius that used to have lunch time sales on their premises.

One of the venues I visited was the headquarters of the Thames Valley Police Force at Kidlington in Oxfordshire. I was invited to set out my wares in the Canteen/Social Club and visited there twice a year. I was always extremely amused when various high-ranking officers made the same joke: "Did these goods fall off the back of a truck?" My response as always the same: "Well, what safer place to bring them than here?" As Henry was travelling again and our son was at prep school, this work was a good outlet for me and kept me busy.

During the time the advert was placed in the local newspaper, I would occasionally receive some unusual requests and some hoax calls. The hoax calls included requests for me to visit London Zoo to pierce the elephants' ears. I usually responded by asking whether they were African or Indian Elephants, before hanging up. Although it was nuisance then, I can appreciate the humour now. The unusual requests were often for piercing various parts of the human anatomy, which, out of courtesy, I will leave to my reader's imagination. Back then these requests were quite shocking, almost taboo. Now they would be very acceptable. Personally, I wouldn't have felt comfortable obliging with my customers' intimate demands. Luckily, my piercing equipment wasn't appropriate for the task, so I had an excuse to turn them down politely.

A GROUP OF MOTHERS

Around this time I noticed that my social life had changed. It just so happened that I only really socialised with other mums who had children at my son's school. If people were invited around, it was normally parents of other children. This was a change of pace. Even though I was generally older than the others mums, it was never an issue. I never felt out of it, which always amazed me.

It all began by holding parties for the children, either at our house or at the houses of the other children. This progressed quite naturally into a situation where we were asking the parents to come over for an evening do. I met some lovely people during this time, a lot of whom I am still in contact with.

THE BUSINESS

In the Mid to Late Seventies, Henry and I started up our own jewellery enterprise. Our company was called H&M Designer Jewellery. The H stood for Henry and the M for Margot, but of course you could read it anyway you chose. We advertised in the Drapers Record, which was a trade magazine for the garment industry. Our goods were either sourced from manufacturers or importers, although some items were imported by us. Besides diamante Swarosvki jewellery, we also specialized in a large variety of gold-plated chains, which were imported from Germany, and pearls, which were imported from Hong Kong and Taiwan. Other items were designed by us, usually pearl and chain necklets.

Henry and I would travel around the country to visit our customers several times during the week. Usually, I would join him on Tuesdays, Wednesdays and Thursdays. We travelled widely visiting our customers in all areas of the South of England, as far up as the Midlands and west to South Wales. Our customers were mainly boutiques specializing in upmarket label outfits. We also supplied our product to dress hire shops that provided evening and ball gowns for special occasions, to which we sold designer "glitz", a type of jewellery that was very much in vogue at that time and worn on TV shows like Dynasty and other popular soap operas.

I enjoyed the travelling as it allowed me to visit various cities and towns across the country that I would otherwise have probably never seen. I always wore an item of our latest jewellery so that, when we walked into our clients' boutiques, the proprietors would immediately be interested in what our latest products were. These meetings would require us to arrive suitably dressed in smart, elegant clothing, as the owners of these establishments were extremely fashion conscious. Henry also dressed in a formal manner, always putting on a smart suit and tie. Our professional image was an important part of our success.

Not long after setting up our business, Henry and I took over the stall at Petticoat Lane. During the war years, when we were living in Crouch End, my parents would do a lot of their shopping there, as it was a venue where we could buy all sorts of food that we enjoyed. With the restrictions of rationing in place, it was always good to use up our limited coupons on food that we really loved. As I was still a reasonably young child, it was such a thrill for me to wander around the stalls. The bustling atmosphere was a lot for a child to take in. There were so many people, so much noise. The mass of people pushing up and down meant that you had to follow the stream of the crowd.

These outings were like an adventure, as amongst all the hustle and bustle Ruth and I would explore all the stalls, and, because we had become quite independent over the years, as most children were in those days, we left the adults to do their shopping with an agreed time and place to meet up later. We would usually meet at Barnett's for a salt beef sandwich with pickles on rye bread. It was great fun watching the sandwich being prepared behind the counter of this enormous butcher and delicatessen.

We would also drift off to Middlesex Street, where you could find our favourite shop, called Mossy Marks, which sold a variety of smoked salmon. The salmon was hand sliced by the most skilled of craftsman. We could watch for hours as he wielded his long serrated knife, producing wafer thin slices of pink succulent salmon. He would always allow his customers to have a taste of their selection before slicing it.

Outside the shop, there was usually an old woman sitting by two barrels of herrings, one of which contained salted herrings, the other pickled herrings. In front of her, she had a trestle table with a wooden board. She would pick out whichever herring had been chosen by her customer, expertly cut it and lay it on some grease proof paper, before smothering it with delicious sliced pickled onions. On the other side of the entrance sat an old man selling bagels from two hessian sacks, not the type of bagels you can buy in any supermarket these days, but small and crisp with a sweetish flavour. The going price for five bagels was only sixpence.

The scene was reminiscent of *Fiddler on the Roof*. Unfortunately, I believe the shop no longer exists, as the Jewish community has gradually moved away to other parts of London. On my most recent visit to Petticoat Lane, I noticed that the stall owners were now mainly Indian, Bangladeshi or Pakistani. Historically, immigration has always altered the feel of a neighbourhood. During the eighteenth century, the Huguenots brought their customs and culture to the East End of London. Now the area has become home to new communities. As I have said, change is the only constant in life.

When we made the decision to take on the stall in Petticoat Lane, Henry and I saw it as a supplement to our business, as the market only functioned on a Sunday. We were able to sell vast amounts of merchandise at higher margins of profit. So, despite the extra effort, it was a profitable venture. During the week, we continued to make our professional visits to the lovely ladies who ran the variety of boutiques and dress hire shops to which we supplied our products.

During my years working with Henry in the Lane, I met people from all over the globe and found it a most fascinating experience. A by-product of this was that we learned to count in quite a few languages, as well as learning a few useful phrases in Japanese, Arabic, and most European languages.

We were regularly visited by a number of Senegalese men based in Paris, who only bought two of our designs but in vast quantities. One design was a topaz necklet, bracelet and earring set. As they were used to bartering, they would always ask for a *cadeaux* in return for their repeat business. We would add a matching ring to their order to satisfy this request. A whole group of these men would come over to Petticoat Lane every four weeks or so and buy the same merchandise. They also went to Middlesex Street, where there were a number of material shops, and bought large bales of certain fabrics. They told us that they sold all these items in a market near Notre Dame in Montmartre. It was exciting to know that our product was being sold in Paris. I liked to imagine elegant Parisian woman strolling down the Champs-Elysees wearing our earrings.

Another item of ours that was very popular was a gold plated Allah pendant that we sold in large quantities, often in the dozens, mainly to people of Middle Eastern origin.

We were also visited by Nigerian "Market Mommas". Many Nigerian women could be found at the market engaging in all sorts of commercial activities. They would brighten up any dull overcast London day with their gloriously multi-coloured outfits. Whenever they wanted to look at an item of ours they would make the request by simply saying, "Bring it me!" I found this high-handed demand quite rude, but had no problem humouring them.

Another feature of Petticoat Lane, although a less appealing one, was the pickpockets. We often warned women not to carry bags hanging from their shoulders but to keep them in front of them so that they were visible at all times. It was not unusual for thieves to cut open a women's bag whilst she stood in front of a stall distracted by the merchandise on show. On several occasions, we returned to our car to find empty purses and wallets that had been thrown underneath.

ISRAEL

When Lee was settled at prep school and life was running pretty smoothly, I thought that it would be a good time to visit Paul, who was living and working in Israel. I had not seen him for several years and felt that it would be good to catch up. I could also use the opportunity to visit my father's siblings, one brother and one sister, who had immigrated to Israel back in 1936.

Paul was working for a travel agent in Tel Aviv. During my visit he put me up with him in his apartment. When he was in his early twenties, he had spent a year in Israel. He showed me the Kibbutz, a collective community, where he had worked during that year.

We stayed with one of the original founders of this wonderful community. She was an amazing woman and told me so much about the struggles they had been through when they had first arrived there during the early 1930s. She described how they had worked to develop the site into a dairy farm and explained how they came to be producing a variety of vegetables and oranges for export on the side. What I found fascinating was the sense of community, a place where one could live from birth to death. The centre of the Kibbutz was devoted to the children, the future of the country.

Everything was owned communally. No one owned their own car; however, there was a car pool, and if someone needed a car they could use one of these vehicles. There was a theatre and a sports facility. Each couple had their own small home, where they could live with their children. If they wished they could cook their own meals, although food was prepared for everyone at the central communal restaurant. They were free to either eat in there or take their portion back to their own home. After completing their education, the older children could choose any career and go to university anywhere in the world funded by the Kibbutz. Whilst I stayed there, I was quite enthusiastic about this communal living, but possibly it was quite an idealized perception on my part.

Whilst in Israel I met my father's sister, Bertha. She had immigrated to Israel in 1935 with her husband, whom she had met when living in Brazil. I also met her daughter, my cousin, who had become a Jehovah's Witness. My aunt was a very interesting woman, highly intelligent and a very gifted needlewoman. In fact, she gave me a very beautiful tapestry, which she made for me whilst I was there. She must have been in her seventies. I believe she lived well into her nineties.

I also met my uncle, Joseph, who had also immigrated to Israel during the 1930s from Germany. He had married someone he met there, meaning that his children were first generation Israeli citizens.

As my son was working for a travel company he had organized some interesting tours for us to Jerusalem, Galilee and the Dead Sea. I took the opportunity to float in the Dead Sea, allowing me to finally enjoy the wonderful experience that I had passed on as a grumpy teenage girl during our travels across America in the 1940s. It was only a seven-day holiday, but I really felt that I had seen so much in such a short time. It was a fantastic break.

CHAPTER SEVEN 1980-1990

BACK TO SCHOOL

As my interest in adult education continued to grow, each summer I would explore the prospectus of Bracknell College to see what would be of interest for the coming year. I realized that I had acquired many practical, creative and homemaking skills but, other than my Spanish, had never ventured into the more academic side of the courses on offer. The subject that continued to interest me was psychology. From time to time, I would buy a book or magazine that contained articles on psychology and, over the previous decade, had started exploring a lot of yoga philosophy and other New Age thinking. So, in 1980, when I saw there was a part-time A-level course offered at the college and realizing that this would be very different to anything I had done since grammar school, I jumped at the chance to enroll.

I was very apprehensive about signing on as the commitment would hold me to a two-year schedule and I was unsure whether I would be able to cope with the curriculum. I continued to work with Henry but, as it wasn't always necessary for me to visit clients with him, I had sufficient time to attend my classes on a Monday afternoon.

At grammar school we used to write compositions. Now we had to write essays. So a book was bought on how to write essays, followed by a book on how to work with statistics, as we would draw all kinds of data from the experiments we were undertaking.

At first, there was an awful lot to get my head around. I remember that our tutor once said to us, as our group consisted mainly of women, "Look at this as if you were working through a recipe!" At the time, this comment helped me relax and calmed any fears I had about how I would cope with this new subject. Now it just makes me aware of how it used to be taken for granted that women were expected to cook all the meals at home and how only the Cordon Blue restaurant chefs were male. In the present, there are so many women working full-time that it is normal for both partners in a relationship to prepare dinner for the family.

In my case, Henry has been cooking our meals and taking care of the weekly shop for at least ten years. He really enjoys it. This has been a bonus for me, as, although I loved cooking and entertaining in my younger days, I find that I can use the extra time available to pursue other interests. I also love it when he calls out, "Dinner is ready!" I don't feel as if he has taken over "my" kitchen, just pleased he has found an interest in something that he can enjoy. Of course, I enjoy it too, as he has become a great cook over the years.

At the end of the first year, in which we had covered areas in human development, speech, cognitive ability, biology, memory and group dynamics, and had started to create our own experiments, the topic of the exams for the following year came up. I informed my tutor that I had only enrolled for my own interest and could see no point in taking the exam; however, she persuaded me that it would be worthwhile attempting it regardless. I told no one other than my classmates that I was taking the examination. I studied diligently and sat the mock examination. To my surprise, I was able to get pretty decent grades.

I usually wrote my essays at about four o'clock on a Sunday morning, as that was the time that Henry went off to Petticoat Lane, and I would naturally wake when he got up and out of bed. I would head downstairs, make a pot of tea, bring it back to bed, surround myself with all my books and writing materials and work till about seven o'clock. I would then prepare my lunch, wake and dress Lee so that I could drop him off at my in-laws before coming back and taking the London Link Bus, which fortunately stopped across the road from our house, all the way to Aldgate in London. I would arrive just after half past nine ready to help Henry at the market stall.

In 1982, I sat my A-level psychology examination. I had continued to enjoy the course and had produced an experiential folder that was reviewed by an external examiner. During my revision period, I haunted the university library in order to acquire as much information as possible. This was before the internet and the age of instant access to information. The results came out in August, and I was delighted to gain a B grade. I know that in these days "A star" is the result to get, but I was very happy to achieve the standard that I did.

I started toying with the idea of applying to study psychology at Reading University. There were a number of women returning to study, who hadn't taken the opportunity earlier in their lives. In the 1980s, there was a law in place that guaranteed the provision of higher education to anyone who had missed out on the opportunity previously. As I had now finished my A-levels, I qualified for this.

As long as I found a university that would have me, my fees would be paid for by the government. I made inquiries and spoke to one of the tutors in the psychology department regarding my chances of being accepted and about what other A-levels would be required. He told me that it was advisable to take another course, preferably one in sociology. The sociology course occupied me for a year; by the time I had completed it, it was 1984.

I had become very friendly with my tutor. We discussed what I would do with a degree, and I mentioned that I was interested in the possibility of becoming a counselor, specializing in working with couples. I applied to Relate, as it is now known, but was told that I was too old to be considered for training. I thought that being in my fifties with the experience of not just one marriage but two, the second of which lasted nearly twenty-five years, would work in my favour during the application process; however, they said that they preferred younger women of about thirty years old. My tutor also felt the need to warn me that, if I were to get a place at the university, I would be that much older when I graduated and then still have to take training to become a therapist.

WEDDING ANNIVERSARY

In November 1980, Henry's parents celebrated their fiftieth wedding anniversary. We decided to have a big family gathering at our house, as we now had sufficient space to accommodate up to a hundred people in our lounge since the addition of the extension in 1973. Instead of having the party on the 30th November, which was the actual date, we decided to bring it forward to the 30th of September, so that we could have the reception outside on our patio, followed by the main meal in the lounge.

To accommodate for this large number of people, we used long folding tables that could seat twenty people. We had serving staff, but I did all the catering. Because we had a large spare refrigerator in the pool hut and a very large freezer in the garage, I was able to prepare a lot of the menu in advance. As Henry's parents both came from large families, there were a lot of Harris and Garcia representatives.

Interestingly, as I write this, I cannot recall whether my father joined us. Around that time he was beginning to withdraw, but was not yet living in the nursing home. Ruth and Jack and their children all came, as well as many friends of Rosie and Mick. It was a wonderful celebration, and the weather was kind to us.

Ten years later, they were fortunate enough to celebrate their sixtieth diamond anniversary. This time round, I didn't feel the need to prove that I could provide a setting and cater for a large amount of friends and family. Instead, we chose a wonderful venue in Sonning, called The Great House. As many of those attending were quite old, we opted for a luncheon and a cream tea. Two of the original bridesmaids, Rosie's nieces, were still living in London and they made a great entrance following the happy couple into the reception. Rosie and Mick received a telegram of congratulations from the Queen and, being staunch royalists, were overjoyed and most proud of it.

MY FATHER

For a time after my mother died, my father managed to keep up his enthusiasm for life and frequently met his friends in the West End of London for coffee and lunch. He was still living in the apartment attached to Ruth's house on Finchley Road and had a housekeeper, who came in daily to tidy up and prepare food for him. He would often enjoy spending an afternoon buying high quality outfits in places such as Aquascutum and other well-known men's stores. He even had a lady friend who used to go out with him for long walks in Hampstead. So, on the surface, it seemed like a good life. We all thought that he was happy, but, around the time that my father reached the age of eighty, this all began to change, and he began to slump into an old age depression.

Maybe it was the loss of my mother; maybe his diabetes was affecting him; maybe, as one tends to do in old age, he had started living in the past, obsessing over his experiences in Germany, such as his detention in Buchenwald concentration camp. As soon as we figured out that something was not quite right, we sought professional help and he was put on medication, which appeared to help for a while.

He came to stay with me during the summer of 1980. Whilst he was staying with us, we were fortunate enough to have some truly glorious weather. Nevertheless, he could no longer bring himself to be happy. I distinctly recall something he said one afternoon when we were sitting on the patio. The sun was shining brightly in a perfect clear blue sky; Lee had a friend staying and they were both playing in the swimming pool. In a melancholic turn, my father turned faintly towards my direction and said, "I should be enjoying this, but I am not." His depression refused him any joy from the lovely scene in front of him. Unfortunately, at that time, I didn't realize that his attitude was a typical representation of the sentiment of a deeply depressed person.

When he returned to London, his doctor prescribed more medication, but he continued to be unhappy. Eventually, he decided he would prefer to move into a nursing home. It was his decision. Perhaps, he felt more secure in that sort of environment. His lady friend continued to go walking with him. Ruth, Jack and I visited on a regular basis and would usually, weather permitting, take him out for a walk or for coffee.

After a while, he felt that he couldn't go outside anymore and withdrew into himself. When I spoke to him on the telephone he would say terrible things, like, "This is the worst day of my life!", or would, rather obsessively, list the various symptoms of discomfort he was currently experiencing.

To make matters worse, the staff and private doctor who attended to my father didn't appear to have much compassion for him. One day Ruth told me that the doctor had suddenly taken my father off of his medication. I discussed this with Joe, our GP. It was Joe's impression that this would have a negative effect on his well-being. He said that the usual practice was to try and keep a patient as old as my father as comfortable as possible, even if that meant giving him the medication to maintain that level of comfort. When I voiced my concerns about the current approach to my father's treatment with Ruth and her husband, they strongly disagreed as the doctor in charge of him was their private doctor. There I was again, the youngest child who couldn't possibly know as much as her older siblings.

Unfortunately, their decision led to a very tragic outcome. My father took his own life. He hanged himself. No one in the nursing home had looked in on him from ten o'clock in the evening until the following morning at six. The rest of my family didn't take the matter further as they had complete faith in the way their private doctor had managed the situation.

My father died in 1981, the winter of which was a particularly cold one. This had affected travelling conditions, and we nearly didn't make it to the funeral, which was held at Bushey Cemetery in Watford. My father had purchased two plots there so that he would be next to my mother. The funeral was arranged for midday.

Henry and I debated as to the best way to get to London, as there had been heavy snowfall during the week and on the previous night. The traffic was moving at a very slow pace, but we thought that, once on the motorway, the road would be clear and we would easily get to Ruth's before they left for the cemetery at eleven thirty. This was a grave misjudgment on our part. It took us thirty minutes just to drive the first half mile. So we then decided it would be better to catch a train and get a taxi to meet the family at Golders

Green. All went well until we arrived into London Paddington. On the approach into the station itself, the train came to a premature stop and we were made to sit for about an hour until the train was allowed to finally draw slowly into the platform. We were fortunate to quickly find a taxi to take us to Golders Green, as the road conditions in London were just as treacherous as in the country. When we finally arrived, the whole family had already left, meaning we had to get back in the taxi and head to Watford on our own. We arrived just in time for the funeral. A very sad day made a whole lot worse by the weather conditions.

One thing I have learned over the years is that nothing lasts forever. There are good times that one needs to embrace and bad times that will pass, as we come to terms with the losses in our lives. Both my parents died in December, my mother three days before my birthday and my father two days before my by birthday. When I was younger, I always felt naturally sad whenever my birthday approached. In the last few years, especially since I passed my seventieth birthday, I have put the loss of my parents into perspective and celebrate the fact that I am still around to enjoy the life that I am blessed with.

RUTH

In January 1985, I sustained a loss which I found almost impossible to come to terms with. My sister Ruth died suddenly whilst on holiday in America. This holiday had been arranged as a family holiday. Ruth and her husband were very friendly with Herman and his wife and always met up for vacations. On these trips to America, they would spend time visiting nieces and other members of the family. This time the arrangement was that Ruth and Leon would fly to Florida to meet up with my cousin Bernice, as well as her brother Seymour and her husband Darwin. Herman and Esther, his wife, also joined them from Los Angeles. They were going to spend two weeks in and around Florida sailing and then fly onto Los Angeles. It was January, the height of the Florida season. Regrettably, the weather was really bad, with frosts and snow, and they were made to change their plans when the entire group caught the flu.

As told to me later by Herman, it appeared that Ruth was the last of the group to become infected with the virus. He noticed on the return flight that she looked really unwell, saying that she was overcome by a violent coughing fit and kept dozing off. When they landed in Los Angeles, Ruth and Leon took a cab to Santa Monica, where their daughter was living. She worked in Los Angeles and was part of the reason for them for making the trip. They arrived at their hotel late in the evening. At about two in the morning, Herman received a phone call from Leon saying that Ruth was worse and that he was unsure what to do. Herman suggested that they call an ambulance and she was admitted to a hospital in Santa Monica.

Unfortunately, her condition deteriorated rapidly. She was pronounced dead six hours later. The medical staff said that she was riddled with cancer, though she hadn't shown any signs during the preceding year of being unwell, other than catching mumps twelve months earlier from her grandson. She had said to me during the year that she felt a little tired, but then she was a very active person, so I didn't think anything odd about it. She had been assessed by their private GP, as Leon and Ruth were very trusting of him, and was given the all-clear.

The sad thing for me is that I will never know what she actually died of, as my late sister-in-law told the hospital that Ruth was Jewish, meaning she wasn't allowed to have a post mortem.

It is impossible to describe my feelings when Henry and I went to the airport and saw the coffin. I could accept my parents' death. It was sad and took its toll on me, but I was aware that it was in the normal order of life. This wasn't the case with Ruth's sudden death. The loss of my sister, the closest of my siblings, was a thoroughly painful experience that took a lot out of me. It was a long time before I had fully come to terms with the reality of it.

During the first few months after Ruth's death, I kept frequently in touch with my brother-in-law. Despite having his three loving daughters to comfort him, I realized how devastated he must have been as their marriage had been a very close one. At that time, he was sixty-eight years old, being ten years older than Ruth. I was very surprised when my brother Jack told me, just three months after the funeral, that he had been told by mutual friends that Leon was seeing another woman and had even been away on holiday with her. I had mixed emotions. I was aware that some men find it difficult when they unexpectedly find themselves alone. This wouldn't have surprised me, as Ruth and Leon's marriage had kept to an old fashioned conception of male and female roles. Leon had been used to Ruth looking after him extremely well. I heard that the woman in question came from a Hungarian background, as Leon's family did. In a sense I understood and, when we spoke, I said that in due course I would like to meet this woman, but ideally sometime after the ceremony of the stone setting, which was to take place the following year. In the Jewish religion, the headstone isn't placed on the grave for twelve months following the burial.

Although there is no obligation to hold an unveiling ceremony, the ritual became popular in many communities toward the end of the nineteenth century. Customs vary, but most have an unveiling ceremony a year after the death.

During the year, we spoke a number of times. I began to realize that he intended to take this woman to Ruth's stone setting, insisting that he had now made a genuine commitment to her. I made one more attempt, suggesting that she didn't attend the ceremony but arrived a little later to join us after the ceremony for the buffet provided by my niece. I assured him that I would really like to meet her but that I didn't feel comfortable with her presence at the ceremony. It meant a lot to me, as I felt that it was a day devoted to my sister's memory and would be as close to a conclusive end to our year of mourning as was possible. I felt it wasn't respectful to her for him to arrive arm in arm with this woman, who he intended to marry. I informed my niece that I wouldn't be attending the buffet as I was too distressed with Leon's choice to bring his new partner. Understandably, Leon's daughters sided with him, and so the outcome was that I not only lost a sister, who I dearly loved, but, from that day onward, I was never invited to any kind of family celebrations that took place with my sister's family.

TRANSACTIONAL ANALYSIS

As the 1980s progressed, I continued to attend my yoga classes, worked with Henry and began to look for various short courses that would aid me in fulfilling my ambition to train as a counselor. Reading University had some courses in bereavement counseling that gave me a useful insight into my reaction to the recent losses I had suffered. I also attended a course on transactional analysis. By briefly describing the basic features of this approach, I would like to show how my acquisition of the knowledge being introduced to me in class coincided with my reaching a particular stage in life, where I was naturally beginning to mature intellectually, and how my perception of myself, and others, was affected by this.

Transactional analysis states that within every relationship there is an interaction between two or more people. Within the interaction a transaction takes place. This can be a transaction of words, deeds, feelings, etc. Transactional analysis is a medium whereby the transaction can be analysed in order that the interaction may be better understood and the relationship enhanced. Transactional analysis is not concerned solely with interpersonal relationships but is also a system designed to help people understand themselves better and to change themselves if they so wish.

Transactional analysis examines human behaviour and relations by attributing certain acts to archetypal Ego-states, of which there are three, the Parent, the Adult and the Child. For this reason it is often referred to as the Parent-Adult-Child (PAC) model.

There is a Child in us all that is sometimes well-behaved, that listens and responds well to the moral guidelines presented to them by their Parent voice; however, the Child can also be spontaneous, uninhibited, living fervently in the present and bearing strong feelings of excitement, rage, grief and many other base instincts. There is also a Parent in us that speaks with the voice of authority and is a personification of the "good behaviour" that we learnt from the figures of authority that provided us with rules to live by in the first place. So the Parent can be seen as consisting of all the "do's and don'ts" that make up the basis of our conscience. This can be a critical, controlling voice, which easily makes us and others feel guilty, or a caring, nurturing self that wants to take care of other people. The third voice is that of the Adult and represents the rational, developing, part of us, which is aware of both Parent and Child but thinks and behaves and makes decisions in a reasonable way. The goal of transactional analysis is to develop the Adult in a healthy, happy way.

To summarize, the Parent is life as we are taught. The Child is life as we feel. The Adult is life as we work it out for ourselves. By analysing and diagnosing the ego-state of a client's behaviour, attitudes and actions, a counsellor can determine the underlying factors that are responsible for unhealthy behaviour. They can use this information, first, to help their client understand why they acted/ felt a certain way and, second, to work towards making sure they won't act in this way again.

I bring this up as, by studying this theory of human behaviour, I really began to think about things in a different light. It helped me understand where I was in my life and why I had acted in certain ways during my past. When you reach a certain age it is natural to start thinking: what is it all about it? It just so happened that this need to evaluate myself, which had begun in the 1970s, correlated with and was refueled by my encounter with these theories in my A-level classes.

MATURITY

We often see the ageing process as a loss of life. This can be hard to stomach and lead to unwanted stress and anxiety. If we look at it as just another part of our development, the future can be seen as a challenge to overcome rather than something to regret. In fact, it can be an exciting prospect, a world bursting with new possibilities for personal growth and for acquiring fresh insight. I have come to think that the benefits of a successful ageing process should be seen as akin to those associated with a career change, in the sense that it is an opportunity to reinvent ourselves.

I have noticed that many women struggle with the process of growing old. For some, attempts to resist the inescapable reality of the menopause hinder what can be an easy passage from youth to maturity. As I look back on my life, I am pleasantly surprised that I now feel fortunate to have had a hysterectomy at the age of forty-two. It seems to have freed me from any preconception that I was entitled to eternal youth. This allowed me to enter a period of post-menopausal zest, which has stayed with me to this day.

With maturity comes the freedom to do and be who you truly are and want to be. Psychologists think of adulthood as consisting of three stages: young, middle and maturity. It may not be the case so much these days, but, for my generation and those that preceded it, a women's young adulthood was often defined by their relationships with the men in their life or by the role that they were supposed to fulfil as a woman, i.e. as a wife or mother. I was first made aware of this on the first day of my psychology A-level course. As a preliminary exercise, our tutor asked us to write down an answer to the question, "Who am I?" I found this very thought provoking. I reflected for a while until I realised that, for the duration of my life up to that point, whenever I had reason to introduce myself I would say that I was someone's daughter, wife or sister. I recall as a young girl that, when someone asked me who I was, I would always say, "Mr Adler's daughter". It hadn't occurred to me that I was a person in my own right, a living, breathing, thinking personal sovereignty. So I wrote, "Margot!" What a revelation!

The course made me appreciate that it was finally time for me to become autonomous. In a sense it was like I was giving myself permission, or an overly belated push, to change. My life as I had known it in my young adulthood was not meant to continue as it was.

Whilst coming to terms with Ruth's death, I became more concerned about my own mortality. I genuinely began to consider the possibility that what had happened to Ruth could plausibly happen to me. What if I had been the one to die? How would I be remembered? I don't think this was a peculiar reaction, in fact I believe it to be quite natural. I began to contemplate that I was no longer a young girl, no longer a young woman. I was fifty-four years old and counting! Although it may sound strange at first, the reality of this simple and obvious truth had previously been obscured from me because, for the past ten to twenty years, I had been living in what I can only describe as a time warp. I had been prevented from reflecting on my true chronological age, as most of the other women I mixed with, namely the mothers of my son's friends and the woman on my psychology course, were at least fifteen years younger than me. It is quite true that we adapt to our surrounding environment. I felt like a much younger woman simply because I was surrounded by much younger women and the majority of my time was occupied attending to things that one would normally do at a younger age.

One day, whilst walking through John Lewis, I experienced something which helped straighten this out. It was something of a Eureka moment; although, it was one which enlightened me to what was at first an uncomfortable truth. As I was busy with my shopping, I caught a glance of myself in a full length mirror. Instead of seeing my young, sprightly self, I was staggered to find an imposter posing in my stead. Even though this strange person resembled me in so many ways, the doppelganger seemed too old to be me, so much so that if they hadn't been wearing the same look of shock and pure disbelief that was currently swelling up and engorging me from the inside, I would never have recognized the person looking back at me. I looked so mature. When had I grown so old?

I think in our mind's eye we cling dearly to that precious image of our younger selves for as long as we can. But there comes a time when we must break free from the domineering prevalence of this youthful mindset if we wish to feel comfortable with our older selves. By doing so, I personally began to feel invigorated, almost born again as a new Margot, who had been hiding away all these years. It was a change which felt so natural and unleashed within me a great affirmation for life. I remember thinking to myself: What can I do to give more meaning to my life than it already had in the present? This enhanced my appetite and enthusiasm for my studies and spurred on my dream of becoming a counselor.

CO-COUNSELLING

For the next couple of years, I continued to attend all kinds of courses including one on co-counselling. Co-counseling is usually practiced in pairs with one person acting as the client and one person facilitating, acting as the counsellor, then they reverse these roles. In every session each person spends the same time in the role of both client and counsellor. This gave me the opportunity to explore both sides of the process.

In 1989, after attending many more short courses, I enrolled on an introduction to psychodynamic counselling, which took place at Reading University. This is where I met the director of the Wokingham and District Counselling Service, who was offering this course in order to enrol prospective counsellors for the next one. I wondered whether she would also tell me that I was too old; however, she encouraged me to send in an application and, further to this, I was asked to submit a short paper on my motivation to become a counsellor. This was followed by an interview with members of the organisations committee, and, to my delight, I was told that I had been accepted. So at the age of fifty-nine, I was going to start on a three year course of study that would change my perception of the human condition forever, as well as giving me a new lease of life. I had no idea what the next few years would bring, but I was really looking forward to this challenge.

ROY

In 1987, at the age of forty-seven, Henry's brother passed away. For about two years prior to his death, there had been a gradual deterioration in his condition. Studies from the 1970s onward revealed that Down's syndrome adults tend to develop Alzheimer-type changes in their brains when they are still young. By the age of thirty, the typical plaques and tangles associated with Alzheimer's are there. Prior to the discovery of antibiotics, those afflicted with Down's syndrome used to die in childhood. As a result of post-Second World War antibiotic treatments, the switch to home care rather than institutional care and the application of heart surgery to correct the congenital effects that affect forty to fifty per cent of Down's syndrome babies, as many as eighty per cent of these individuals are living to the age of fifty or greater.

In Roy's case, it was very sad to witness his deterioration, and initially it wasn't picked up on by the GP. He had always been very independent, going daily to a work centre for the disabled and taking two buses to get there. He used to enjoy wandering around Reading and knew many people around town to speak to. He enjoyed going into travel agents to pick up travel brochures. He went on holiday with his parents on a regular basis. In fact, in 1963, Henry and I took him and my son to Las Palmas, and we all had a great time.

He loved watching the *Incredible Hulk* on television and enjoyed imitating the character, as he changed from an ordinary man into this enormous weird-looking giant whenever he was made angry. We first noticed that something wasn't right when he took the wrong bus to get to work. This was soon followed by other instances of memory loss and confusion. At first, whenever he became aggressive, we thought that he was just imitating the Incredible Hulk, but, eventually, we realised that he was suffering, as his condition had deteriorated.

It was a very difficult time for the family. Henry was often called out during the night to help his parents manage with Roy, as they were both in their early eighties by this time. Eventually, in his final months we were unable to cope with the situation and found a private nursing home to care for him, where he remained for about six weeks. During his time there, he was always accompanied by a member of the family until he passed away.

LEE AT UNIVERSITY

My youngest son had decided to go to Reading University in 1988, taking a course in computer science. At the time he was also very involved with his electronic music and had his Yamaha electronic organ installed in our lounge. In fact, Henry and Lee frequently played duets, with Henry playing his baby grand piano. I loved listening to the two making music. For me, it is definitely one of the highlights of that period.

Aside from the organ, Lee had started a small business buying some items for computers at sales and selling them on to other computer enthusiasts at school, at University and at a computer club he frequented.

We made a deal that he should treat our house as university-style lodgings. If he wanted to come back for a meal, I would have prepared enough for him to join us. If not, I would simply leave it in the microwave oven, and he could eat whenever it suited him. This seemed to work well during the three years he was at the university. When he graduated he was fortunate to get a position with a local company, for whom he had worked during his summer breaks from the university.

Two years later he left home, as he was in a position to buy a small house in Berkshire. Henry found it quite difficult to understand why he wanted to leave home at the age of twenty-two, probably because Henry had not left, or even considered the possibility, until he and I married at the age of twenty-nine. I didn't feel the same at all, as I came from a family that had dispersed when I was young. This meant that I didn't experience the empty nest syndrome as some mothers do. To be honest, I was more than ready to enjoy the next stage of my life.

I was very aware that there were differences in the way that Henry and I saw the world. Because of our different developmental experiences, our worldviews were very different. Despite caring deeply for one another, our patterns of attachment caused us some issues at various times. Henry had a strong sense of duty and loyalty towards his parents, which was a very admirable trait, but what he found difficult was being able to create a boundary of self, where he could make choices that didn't have to take his parents into account.

CHAPTER EIGHT 1990-2000

TRAINING

Before I embark on the story of my training and subsequent career as a counselor and psychotherapist, I would like to clarify the distinction between the two and why I sometimes refer to counseling and sometimes therapy.

*"**Counselling** works with conscious difficulties, anxieties or distress; **Psychotherapy** looks more deeply into the underlying causes of our inability to live life as fully as we would like. In both cases the aim is to help you identify, and change if necessary, those behaviours and modes of thinking that are contributing to your current unhappiness."* – Bridget Christiana Seager

During the 1980s, the counselling profession was only just emerging. It had originally been a pastoral listening support provided as part of or in conjunction with various churches. As well as this there were many social workers who were developing the same sorts of skills in their work which would later be taken up by the counselling profession. During the 50s and 60s and 70s, there was a surge of therapists who, despite their analytical training, were moving toward utilising these new ways of dealing with their client's problems.

In January 1990, I started my three-year part time training course to qualify as a counsellor. What I didn't realise at the time was that this marked the beginning of the most fascinating period of my life, one that continues to the present. I feel that the last twenty-two years have been demanding in the most satisfying and exhilarating of ways and represent the biggest learning curve I have encountered since early childhood. I have learned so much about human behaviour and continue to do so that my life is never dull. There is nothing more interesting than people; ergo, there is no job more satisfying than counselling.

There were twenty students signed up on the course, one man and nineteen women. These days more men are training to become therapists and counsellors, but essentially the ratio still favours more females than males in this profession. We were divided into two experiential groups and remained with these same nine people for the entire three-year course. I felt that the experiential group was an essential part of the learning process, as it allowed us to scrutinize ourselves through the feedback we received from the others. We were also advised to keep a personal journal of our experience of the group and to focus on how our perception of ourselves was transforming over time. I believe one of the most important lessons I learnt was that we cannot rescue others, that we can only be who we are and that who we are in the present is influenced by how we were in our family of origin. We can change ourselves, but cannot change another.

Naturally, I made a number of close friends, as we saw each other every week for three years. Many of these women continue to be part of my life. As many of my classmates were as much as twenty-five years younger than I was, I feel that the relationship I have with them is rather maternal. I see them as the daughters I would love to have had.

The course took place every Monday evening from seven o'clock until ten o'clock. Each year was broken up into three terms with long holiday breaks. We also had three training weekends a year, where a particular topic, such as bereavement, relationships, pathology or sexuality, was worked through in depth. Most of these weekends took place at a convent located in Cold Ash, east of Newbury, which was a residence for retired nuns. It was a peaceful environment, a place withdrawn from the world, where one could attend to mental activity in a relaxed and delightful setting. The icing on the cake was the wonderful home cooking prepared by the nuns. The weekend would comprise of lectures, skills training, roleplaying and group work. I always looked forward to these training weekends as I enjoyed being surrounded by such a diverse group of people who, regardless of their backgrounds and other differences, all shared a common interest in training to be counsellors.

At the end of the first year, we had to write papers on various topics. Our progress was judged by our tutors as to whether we were ready to start seeing a maximum of two clients under strict supervision. Supervision is a mandatory requirement for any accredited counsellor or psychotherapist course. It protects the best interests of the clients, as well as supporting the counsellor.

I saw my first client in February 1991. Needless to say, I was extremely anxious to get everything right. I had concocted a mental image of how a counsellor ought to dress and would need to present herself and tried to adhere to this a much as possible. At that time it was a middle class profession, comprising of a high percentage of middle aged women garnered from the teaching, nursing and social work professions. Sometimes women whose children had left home or who had done voluntary service in their churches were also drawn to the profession to improve their knowledge and skills. I think that I was the only person on the course who was self-employed and still in business. I was also the oldest.

For the first meeting, I wore a pleated skirt, twin set and pearls. I was immaculately dressed, looking very proper. I knew in advance that this person, who was soon to become my first ever client, had previously been assessed by an experienced counsellor in order to judge their suitability. This provides the experienced counsellor with a general idea of the presenting issues before handing the client over to someone less experienced. It also gives the novice a means to prepare and an initial guideline as to what area to focus on. During the session, the brief is simply to listen and make appropriate responses. When it was over, the task was to write up the notes of the process and content, and bring it to the weekly supervision group for discussion. I was so terrified that I would forget something important that I went into the session with an A4 pad of paper and made prolific notes, which wasn't what had been recommended in class.

I have now developed a very good recall of what has been discussed during a session with a client. I am lucky to be able to refer to a photographic recall of the story that has been told to me, as I see the story in the form of pictures, a very useful skill. Immediately after a session, I write some brief notes, from which it doesn't take much to recall what was mentioned at a later date. It is often the case that clients return for more counselling after a few years. I am able, by looking at their assessment, to immediately recall their story. This enables me to see people for short contracts, and, if or when something else happens that they feel they would like me to work through with them, most find it easier to return to the same counsellor as their history has already been familiarised.

In the present, I work mainly with the short term model and I am identified as an integrative counsellor. My core training was in psychodynamic theory.

The basic technique and strategy of the psychodynamic approach is free-association. It is helpful to think of free association as bearing the tagline: the past repeats in the present. It holds that whatever comes to mind from the past is significant and somehow connected to current life issues. In this way, the approach can be very useful for understanding why a client behaves as they do. Thus psychodynamic theory can be considered a useful frame of reference for conceptualising clients and for helping clients think about themselves in a far more positive light.

I soon became more relaxed and began seeing other clients. Even for a novice counsellor it is better to see more than just one client initially, as it is easy to become emotionally involved if your focus is concentrated on one person. For this reason, the supervision is such an important aspect of the process.

During the second year, we looked at pathology, adolescence, and other aspects of human development and behaviour. There was also an introduction to couple counselling, which I found so interesting that I opted for more training in that area. As well as what was taught on the course, I looked for workshops on topics I felt would contribute to my core training. In particular, I looked at the practical basis of supervision because, although I knew the importance of it, I didn't appreciate or feel that I fully understood the process. The supervisor who had been assigned to me for the first year hadn't felt the need to explain it in detail. In many ways the students were quite infantilised. This was one of the reasons I was unhappy with the manner in which our supervision was carried out. But it wasn't just the supervision that was like this. The same level of condescension could also be seen elsewhere on the course, in tutorials and seminars.

The training model and the tutors, who facilitated the training model, were quite analytical, with a number of them proudly proclaiming that they had been in analysis for many years. The facilitator of our group was much like this. During our weekly meetings, I found it extremely irritating that everyone was reluctant to get involved in discussion and that the facilitator did almost nothing to encourage us. After the lecture, we gathered into our separate groups for a seminar but would often just sit there in silence waiting for someone to pick a topic or for the first person to say something. To my annoyance no one spoke up. I felt it was a waste of precious time as I had lots to say, but didn't wish to be the first one to speak. I always thought that the earlier part of the evening merited more discussion and was keen to hear what some of the others had to say about the lecture.

I can recall one particular evening where the silence had gone on for at least ten minutes. That evening I happened to be sitting next to the facilitator. Interrupting our customary silence, she turned to me and said, "Margot! Why are you fidgeting so much?" To this, I just burst out laughing. I felt like a naughty child who had been caught misbehaving. Obviously, my response was not that of a naughty child, and so I pointed out that in my view the reluctance of the group to start any kind of meaningful discourse was a waste of time and that this was what had triggered my "fidgety" demeanour. Her response was typical of a person who had been in analysis. She began to question me in front of the whole class, "Why are you being so aggressive? What is making you feel angry?" Anyway, this finally appeared to get the group going. To me it felt like I was engaged in some kind of Adult/Child relationship, which made me particularly uncomfortable, considering I was the oldest one there.

Our group was an interesting bunch of people. There was the quiet one, the knowledgeable one, the aggressive one, the rescuer, the victim, the persecutor and the entertainer. I think over the years our roles changed somewhat, as we gained insight into our own way of relating to others. The main change I noticed in myself was that, instead of being either the entertainer or the good girl, I began to react in a more measured manner. I began to listen more and learnt when it was appropriate to say something. I also learnt that silence is golden and grasped the importance of taking the time to thoroughly think before I spoke.

NIRVANA SPA

I continued to go to my health club, Nirvana Spa, which was now conveniently situated on the route from our home in Sonning to the counselling centre in Wokingham. I would either visit the club on my way there or on my way back. I made many friends at the health club, some of whom are still good friends in the present.

One morning during the 1990s, when I turned up for my early morning swim, I overheard some talk in the changing room that Princess Diana was using our club's facilities for the day. As I entered the pool, I was pleasantly surprised to see an extremely beautiful young woman, matching the Princess of Wales' description, engaged in an impressive front crawl. I must add here that being a private health club there were rarely more than five or six people in the pool at any given time. I imagine this is why she chose our club, as it would allow her the peace to swim with relative privacy.

There was a woman at our club who was consumed by a severe fear of drowning. This never deterred her from swimming, and she could be found in the pool several times a week; although, her swimming routine was limited to paddling up and down in the shallow end. Her fear would not allow her to attempt anything more adventurous than that. She was a very sweet woman and we would all try and help her conquer her fear by offering support and advice. It just so happened that this woman was in the pool at the same time as Princess Diana. Diana must have noticed that she was in some discomfort and so approached her with a friendly smile and spent ten minutes or so speaking with her. Princess Diana really was a lovely person, and her untimely death was a great loss.

WORK, WORK, WORK

Every so often, I would join Henry to visit our customers, but not as frequently as I had done previously. Whilst I was training, I still didn't see myself turning counselling into a career because, despite the enjoyment I gained from the process, I was far from confident as to how well I would manage in the long term; however, by 1993, I was seeing about six clients a week. In training we were learning to work with couples, something which proved to be very useful for reflecting on our own relationships.

In the present, I see many couples, and, though couple work is more demanding, there is always a great sense of satisfaction when the outcome is positive. This doesn't necessarily mean that the couple stay together, but that the separation is not as acrimonious as sometimes happens. When there are children involved, as is frequently the case, it is often the children who are affected the most by the experience of their parents' divorce. Some children find the whole affair deeply disturbing, and it can have lasting implications that affect their future development. Children often feel that the parent who is leaving is abandoning them because he or she doesn't love them anymore. They cannot see that the separation is just the natural end and the final stage of their parents' marriage now that it has broken down.

MARGOT'S PRIVATE PRACTICE

By the end of 1993, I had completed my course and gained my qualifications for psychodynamic counselling. I had seen quite a few clients, but, at that stage of the training process, the main aim was to practise in-depth therapy, meaning that we would hold longer sessions than was perhaps usual. So, whilst I had accumulated the hours necessary for my qualification, I had probably only seen about fifteen clients. After the course I continued seeing clients at the counselling centre. I was also on the committee by now, as the student representative, and was generally greatly involved within the agency, attending further workshops on a variety of topics.

At the same time, I attended further training in anger management and brief therapy. In 1993, brief therapy was just being recognised as an effective intervention, and so, after attending a seminar, I carried out more research into this way of working and considered the possibility of using it in the future. The advantages of brief therapy were numerous. The most obvious is that a lot of people interested in seeking therapy struggle to find the time to spend weeks and weeks undertaking an in-depth analysis. Brief therapy concerns itself with helping its clients arrive at specific issues more directly, rather than letting them flounder on going nowhere fast. Brief therapy was something that I really took to. The most important part of adapting to this approach was studying human dynamics, i.e. learning how people tend to behave in their life cycle.

For the next two years, I worked towards my accreditation for becoming an accredited member for the British Association for Counselling and Psychotherapy (BACP). It was the final step in becoming a counsellor and would mean that I was nationally recognised as a professional healthcare practitioner. I received my accreditation certificate in November 1995, and to say that I was delighted would be a colossal understatement. I was alone in the house when the post came and, clutching my accreditation in hand, just ran and ran around the house with great joy, dancing and shouting, "Yes! Yes! I have really done it." The adrenaline rush was fantastic.

I was now ready to set up in private practice. I decided to work from my home as I had several spare rooms that I could choose from, as well as a downstairs study that could be used as a waiting room. We were also fortuitous to have plenty of room for parking in the driveway.

MARGOT'S CLASSES

Whilst I had been working towards my accreditation, I had offered my services to Nirvana Spa health club as a stress management therapist. I felt I was more than competent for this role as I had acquired a great deal of experience practicing yoga and had a comprehensive understanding of a wide variety of relaxation and breathing exercises. The club was bringing in a wide variety of outside practitioners, such as osteopaths, physiotherapists and chiropodists, to deliver onsite services for its members. After a few preliminary meetings with the manager, I persuaded him that my services would be of value and I was duly allocated one of their rooms to use for my meetings. I ran a six-session programme.

I continued taking classes at Woodley Hill House. I had recently taken another word processing course, as it was apparent that being computer literate was the way to go.

I regularly used the photo copying facilities at Woodley Hill House for copying any material that I needed. One afternoon, as I was making some copies of a document on assertiveness, a woman, who was waiting behind me and next in line for the copying machine, asked me whether I was one of the college's tutors. I replied that I wasn't but suggested that I probably looked familiar as I had attended so many classes there over the last thirty years. She told me she was asking because she had noticed that the copies I was making were related to assertiveness training. I informed her that I ran a programme at a health club and that these copies were for a number of my clients from there. She was a very pleasant lady and seemed to be very happy to have run into me. I found out that she was the Head of Studies at the college and her delight at finding me was attributed to the fact that she was in need of someone to take a Saturday workshop, titled: "Assertiveness for Women", as the person who usually took the class was off sick. I said that I had never delivered a workshop to a group but that, over the years of my counselling training, I had frequently been part of a group experience and was more than capable of leading a group. We organised a meeting to discuss this further, with the outcome that, a few weeks later, I delivered the workshop.

The feedback from the participants was so positive that the Head of Studies asked me whether I could give the class on a regular basis, and whether there were any other workshops that I could think of that might be of interest. So I planned two six-week courses, "Anxiety and Stress" and "Communication in Relationships".

I felt an overwhelming sense of completion, having started courses there shortly after I married in 1962, to be invited back to deliver my own workshop. It was a case of pupil-turned-teacher and gave me the most wonderful feeling.

Then the Head of Studies from Woodley Hill House invited me to take part in a government initiative on retirement, where I was asked to speak about the possible psychological effects on prospective retirees. There were many other contributors who spoke on subjects such as pensions and IT skills, all in order to help manage the transition into retirement.

One day, a couple of years later, when I was in my health club, a woman approached me who I didn't fully recognise, although her face looked vaguely familiar. She said she was desperate to speak with me as she had attended the retirement course and it had had a hugely positive effect on her retirement. She said it really made her reflect on her situation, leading her to make a number of decisions that had helped her establish a quality of life in the present that she had never imagined possible. I was very touched by this and thanked her for her kind words.

FREEPHONE SERVICES

During 1996, Lee, who was working for an American telecoms company, came home one day and said that he had been given a plastic card with a Freephone number to be used as a means of accessing confidential counselling if he was ever experiencing emotional difficulties. This service was available to every single worker at his firm and was my first introduction to Employee Assistance Providers (EAP's).

EAP was a fantastic scheme that had originated in America. It provided the services of counsellors to corporations as part of the health care package for their employees. Instead of keeping in-house counsellors, a Freephone service is established, meaning that each individual employee is only ever a phone call away from receiving professional help. These cases were short term cases. The employers were willing to pay for a limited amount of sessions. If I hadn't trained in brief therapy, I wouldn't have been so successful with this kind of work. The clients I would see were healthy people reacting to life events. A lot of these clients just needed someone to voice their concerns to, which were mostly to do with relationships or stress at work. They would see me for a few sessions, and for most of their concerns this was sufficient to gain insight into the causes of the issues presented and resolve the situation. If they ever needed me again, they could contact the EAP Company and ask for me if they wished to do so.

I approached the company that was offering the EAP service, at that time they were called EAR, European Assistance Resources, and signed a contract with them as an affiliate counsellor. They were a good company to be associated with and offered periodic training in a variety of skills that were extremely useful when working with clients over such a limited number of sessions. I also attended a number of seminars that dealt with debriefing people who had experienced traumatic events.

On one of these training events, there was a representative of the Employee Assistance Provider Association, who was offering special terms for a two-year membership to any of the counsellors attending. I thought that this was a useful association to join, as all the major EAP providers were members. Through attending quarterly meetings, I subsequently ended up becoming an affiliated counsellor for another six major EAP providers. My services were outsourced to a variety of global companies, such as Oracle, Microsoft, IBM, and many more.

Initially, when I started working with these providers, the referrals were always via telephone. If I accepted the client, the relevant documents were posted to me, and subsequently I would have to return the completed documents in the same manner. Some companies will still contact via telephone to this day, although several operate via email. Often there is an online portal, where the rest of the transaction, feedback and other notes are completed online. In fact, some companies are now offering purely online counselling. I choose not to get involved with this type of contact as I strongly believe in the value of face-to-face contact. Creating a relationship with your clients face-to-face is for me the joy of the work. That is not to say that I don't appreciate why a younger generation of people, who have become used to social interaction through the medium of instant messenger and texting, might prefer to proceed online. However, I think that this immediacy of communication and instant access to a virtual world, where one can hide behind an avatar on a computer screen, presents problems for younger people and leads to them lacking the social skills necessary for healthy interaction with others.

One thing that I hope has come across in this description of my life as a counsellor is the wide variety of options open to a qualified counsellor in plying their trade. Within the practise I could see such a variety of styles of counselling, which have proven to be a continuous source of motivation for me. The awareness that I could stay within one career and have such a diversity of experiences, with clients from all kinds of backgrounds, with all sorts of problems, was very appealing to me. I knew I had finally found a profession that would keep me intellectually stimulated for many years to come.

A SPECIAL FRIEND

I have loved and continue to love the counselling work I do. The relationship between counsellor and client is unique. In essence it is a meeting of strangers, where one stranger confides in another, sharing their most intimate thoughts. Most of the time, we discuss concerns that my clients aren't willing to talk about with their friends. Sometimes this is because they don't wish to burden them, but often it is because their close friends and family may be the cause of their distress.

I have heard a multitude of peoples' stories, which are always interesting, sad and, nine times out of ten, centred on their closest relationships. The privilege of being allowed to share a person's thoughts, feelings and fears is one that I am proud to experience. Every time we embark on the road to their recovery, I get to witness the delight my clients' feel as they overcome their troubles and move forward with their lives. Meeting a new client is like opening a new book, a mystery novel full of suspense. My role can be likened to searching for the clues in their story to aid them in rewriting their script.

All of my clients have been important to me and many of them have taught me so much; however, there is one incredibly special person, who with her sister's permission, I would like to mention. I found her to be the bravest and loveliest person I have ever had the chance to meet. Her name was Jules and, when she first came to see me, I was dumfounded by how beautiful she was. She was tall, stylishly dressed, had luscious red hair and a charming smile. The beauty of her appearance was matched by her fantastic sense of humour and genial personality.

Her presenting issue was that she was pregnant at thirty-five years old and had become unhappy in her marriage. She was a successful professional, working for a global company. In her twenties, she had worked as a Red Coat at Butlins. Despite the severity of her troubles, her sense of fun was always present as we sat down to begin our sessions.

During her pregnancy, she was constantly nauseous, which didn't abate following the birth of her son. When her baby was about one-week old, she began to suffer from excruciating headaches as well. Her doctors scanned her head and diagnosed her with an aggressive form of brain cancer. It was said she had only three months to live.

At that time I had continued to counsel her via telephone. I remember her saying to me, "I am going to beat this. I cannot die; I have just had a baby." She had an operation to remove the malignant tumour and underwent radiotherapy. Due to her strong will and love of her son, she eventually saw signs of recovery; although, the long term prognosis didn't inspire too much hope.

Nevertheless, Jules kept on living with the same enthusiasm for life that she always had. When she next came see me, she was wearing the most fabulous red wig and, as usual, was impeccably dressed. For a while, things were looking good, and she returned to work. After four years, she held a party to celebrate her four-year survival and invited me to join her on the occasion along with her closest friends and family.

Unfortunately, two years later, the tumour returned. As she endured further treatment, I spoke with her regularly on the phone. She had recently moved out of the area, so her sister chauffeured her when she came to visit. It was during December and, as Jules had always loved Christmas and there was a house near-by particularly dolled up in extravagant bright lights and all kinds of miscellaneous Christmas paraphernalia, she took a detour to have a quick peak at it.

She passed away when her son was eight years old. I attended the funeral, for which she had planned the whole service. It was an uplifting celebration of a truly inspiring woman. A projector displayed an exhibition of photographs from different stages of Jules' life, in all of which she looked stunningly beautiful. The eulogies all confirmed what a wonderful person she was. The only flowers requested at the funeral were lilies, as Jules simply adored lilies; each person attending was invited to place a lily at her resting place.

CREATIVITY

As the decade flew past, I began to feel that I had been neglecting my creative side, as I had spent so many years ingrained in my studying. I suddenly felt like I needed a change of pace. Initially, I began in my usual manner of signing up for a short course. This time it was a beginner's guide to creative embroidery. I had always enjoyed different types of crafts and had been knitting and making tapestries for years. I had dabbled in painting with both acrylics and oils but found the clearing up stage to be too time-consuming. The course in embroidery introduced me to a new way of working that allowed me to paint with threads. It was such a joy!

To my surprise, the tutor encouraged me to join the Embroiderers' Guild. I had seen their beautiful work at various exhibitions and tried to reason with her that this was for experts, not for me. Nevertheless, I did join the Reading Embroiderers' Guild, attended many workshops and immersed myself in such a wonderful world of design.

In 1998, two years before the millennium celebrations, there was a notice in the Sonning parish magazine for volunteers to help with a project oriented towards making a wall hanging for the village church to commemorate the village and its people at the advent of the new millennium. The hangings were designed by a very talented woman, who lived on the next road down from our house. They depicted the life of the village during the four seasons of the year. A group of us spent the next two years meeting on Wednesdays and Thursdays until the project was completed. We brought in our own material, including some that I had cut from my own curtains.

I think that the reason I was drawn to return to my creative streak was based on the Jungian, as well as the Hindu concept, of internal balance. It can be described as centring oneself. Jung suggested that in order to be a balanced person it is necessary to attend to all the functions that make the complete balanced individual. These are the cognitive, the physical, the creative and the spiritual. By "spiritual", Jung does not necessarily mean formal religion, but more an awareness of the present, such as the beauty of a cloud formation, a sunset or a piece of music that touches us. The Hindus think of this as seeing ourselves as a house with four rooms. In order to gain a balance we need to go into each room each day and air them.

"Everyone is a House with four rooms. Most of us tend to live in one room most of the time but, unless you go into every room, every day, even if only to keep it aired you are not a complete person." – Rumer Godden

I believe this was the case with me. I had neglected the creative side of my Self and a general feeling of imbalance had drawn me back towards art.

CHAPTER NINE 2000-2012

THE RETURN(S)

At the turn of the millennium, I returned to Germany and my place of birth, Kassel, at the invitation of the town's mayor. After the fall of the Berlin Wall and the break-up of the communist regime, an influx of Jewish people, numbering about eight hundred, had arrived from Russia and settled in Kassel. This had prompted the mayor to organise a reunion for any Jewish people who had been displaced from the town during the 1930s. I accepted this invitation; however, it wasn't my first return, as two years earlier Henry and I had visited the town whilst in Germany on business.

In 1998, Henry and I travelled to Germany as one of our main suppliers was based there. We thought it would be a good opportunity for a short holiday. Now that it was nearly sixty years since my family had escaped, I felt ready to return. It seemed unlikely that I would come across anyone who had been involved in the persecution of the Jews. I could safely assume that the people I would encounter whilst walking the streets, eating in restaurants, visiting the museums etc. would have been children like myself during the war and would have had nothing to do with what happened. In fact, I had read a book that explored how the children of the perpetrators of the holocaust had been greatly affected as they grew up and learnt of their parents' activities.

We drove to the manufacturer, taking a scenic route which followed the path of the Rhine across Southern Germany. It was early summer and the vineyards were just beginning to blossom. We took a lovely boat trip, devoured lots of German cuisine, completed our work obligations and then continued on toward Kassel.

Prior to making the trip, we had contacted the town council for information, and, in discussing the reason for our visit, they told us that any Jewish people born in Kassel were invited to stay as guests of the town, with travelling and hotel expenses paid for. As we had planned to drive, we didn't take them up on their offer of paying for our travelling costs, but allowed them to arrange the hotel for us.

Once we had settled in the hotel, we set out to explore the town. I couldn't wait to find the place where I was born. Although large parts of the town had been destroyed during the war, the town had been rebuilt in such way that it looked almost exactly how I remembered. I was utterly determined to seek out every single place that I could think of. It amazed me that I was able to recognise them after such a long time. It was wonderful to go back after all those years and walk the same streets I did as a little girl; this time with a completely different perspective. How different little Margot was from the woman I am today.

Whilst we were strolling around, I was particularly flattered when someone came up to me to ask for directions. I suppose I didn't look much like a tourist, especially since I was able to reply in German.

The second trip was different to the first in many ways. First of all, this time I went on my own. The invitation was for both me and my husband, but, unfortunately, Henry's mother's condition had been deteriorating for some time and he felt that he couldn't leave her. For me this was a once-in-a-lifetime opportunity to meet a group of people I wouldn't otherwise ever have the chance to meet, who all shared a common thread with me. Although we had, quite literally, been dispersed all over the globe, we had each begun our journey at the same junction: we had all experienced the same fear, terror and loss that had ruptured our humble community all those years ago.

Second, the town had planned all sorts of events and activities. There were concerts, outings to various places of interest and receptions laid on for all the guests, who had travelled from all over the world to attend this unique occasion.

It just so happened that I had already been in correspondence with one of the guests who was also coming from the UK. I had made contact after reading an article in a newspaper, several years prior to this event, concerning the children who had arrived in the UK as part of the Children Transport Scheme. There were others there from the UK, many of whom had been part of this initiative. They spoke of their experiences, of which some were good, others not so fortunate. Many of them were still affected by the trauma of having to leave their parents behind. It was clear that the sadness of never seeing their parents again had stuck with them throughout their adult lives; for some these emotions only intensified now that they were back in their childhood town. Other guests came from as far as South America, Australia, the United States, Israel, Argentina and Brazil. The awareness that we were, in fact, the lucky ones, the ones who had survived, gave us a common bond.

I had brought quite a number of photos of my brothers and sisters, as I hoped that I might meet someone who had been at school with them. My efforts weren't in vain. I met someone, now living in Argentina, who recognised my brother and sister from their class at school.

I have attached a picture taken of the whole group by a reporter, who accompanied us throughout the week. He wrote a daily report in the newspaper, describing our activities and recording the observations we made of how this reunion was affecting our memories of the past. There was a German woman who asked us to record our memories for a living history, and we were given a number of books relating to the past history of the town. One particularly haunting read was a hugely thick book containing the names and fate of all the Jews of Kassel between the years of 1933-1945. A very sobering document tabling the names of all the people living in Kassel during that time, their profession, where they resided and where they ultimately perished, and in what year. It was from reading this book that I discovered the details of where my cousins, my aunt, my grandfather and my girlfriend Rita came to the end of their lives.

The group went on several outings using a couple of coaches. On one of these outings, a man asked me whether I had noticed a couple of men on each coach who were not mingling with the rest of the group. I replied that I had, but hadn't deemed it to have any significance. He told me that these men were security, "riding gunshot", because there was still a right-wing faction in Germany and our hosts didn't wish to put us at risk.

I have not returned to Kassel since that occasion. Over the duration of my two trips there, I learnt a lot about the past and recent history of the town and, other than reflecting on what it might have been like to grow up there in less hostile times, I felt that I finally had closure on that part of my early life.

POSTTRAUMATIC STRESS

My private practice was thriving. I continued to have a variety of clients referred to me from various sources. I began to work with people who were suffering from experiences of traumatic events, as I had previously attended a number of training courses on managing posttraumatic stress. One definition of posttraumatic stress is: "The development of characteristic symptoms following a psychologically distressing event outside the range of normal human experience". This sums up the crux of this kind of work perfectly. You are dealing with the reactions of normal people to abnormal events. It can influence an individual's feelings about themselves and others, meaning that their partners and families can be caught up in changes which are impossible for them to understand. Apart from causing marital stress and the breakdown of relationships, it can lead to problems at work, ill health and, sometimes, the development of deeper and more disturbing symptoms.

In a strange way, perhaps somewhat like the natural intuition that compels drivers to slow down at road accidents, I found it intellectually fascinating to share in the harrowing experiences of these people; however, the true fulfilment of this work was the challenge of helping these people return back to the normal swing of things.

Many of my cases consisted of shop workers who had been held up at gunpoint. These included robberies at petrol stations, local shops and small supermarket chains. Following the 9/11 terrorist attack in New York, I was asked by one of the EAP companies to see a woman who had been working in the second tower when the events of that dreadful day occurred.

I first met her about four weeks following the event. Initially, I visited her at her home because she was unable to drive and didn't feel up to leaving the house. Following her return from New York three weeks after the event, despite bearing the physical effects of the ordeal, caused by walking down forty-eight flights of stairs and then running away from the collapsing buildings, she had felt as if she was coping quite well. So, seeing no reason not to, she returned to her office in the city.

As she walked in and saw her colleagues sitting there working, as if nothing had happened, she was overwhelmed with an acutely severe sense of anxiety and suffered a panic attack. In the debriefing we explored the cause of this attack and discerned that it was anger. She was angry that her colleagues seemed oblivious and grossly indifferent to what she had experienced. This experience was something she would have to live with for the rest of her life, whilst their lives would continue unaffected, as normal.

On the first meeting, I spent two hours with her. It is amazing how, ten years after our initial session, I can still recall the account that she gave me in minute detail. I can picture it almost as if I was there. I think this has something to do with the fact that it was still so fresh in her mind and had taken such a significant hold over her.

She began by explaining why she had been in New York and that she was attending a meeting on the forty-eighth floor. She had been waiting on her own in a separate office from her colleagues, where a buffet of hot drinks and cakes were laid out, when she saw the first plane hit the North Tower. She noted how much this sight seemed unreal to her, more like seeing a movie than witnessing a real-life event. She was overcome by disbelief and had to call over to her colleagues to verify the reality of what she was seeing. Was this really happening?

Next, she remembers the vibration from above as the tower she was in was hit. She decided, with a friend, to get out of the building as quickly as possible and so started to make her way down the forty-eight flights of stairs that stood between her and the ground floor. She made this decision despite hearing a message on the Tannoy System instructing everyone to stay in their offices. Having disposed of her computer, briefcase and shoes on reaching the twentieth floor, she finally made it all the way down to the ground floor, where she was met by a number of firemen, who were instructing everybody to move out onto the plaza and rest there, as a refuge centre had been set up. Feeling unsafe, she felt compelled to get as far away from the building as possible. Despite her complete exhaustion, she hurried down the road, still with her friend, and remembers seeing the shiny, red fleet of stationary fire engines parked along both sides of the road.

Suddenly, there was a huge roar as the first building collapsed and everybody started running frantically past her. Instinctively, she ran into the nearest doorway and became separated from her friend. As she stood in the doorway, shielding herself from the oncoming wave of dust, smoke and falling debris, more and more people piled in on top of her with little knowledge or regard of her and her well-being. Everyone was in a state of panic and she felt that she was going to suffocate. Plunged in complete darkness and with the pressure of those on top of her weighing down on her, she began to think, "I am going to die here!" She couldn't remember how long she was stuck there. The dust and smoke were slowly, excruciatingly asphyxiating her.

Sometime later she became aware that the others who had crammed in on top of her had moved on. Realising she was still alive, her thoughts turned to the whereabouts of her friend. Amid the darkness, she left the doorway and continued to walk away from where the two towers had recently stood, until she caught sight of an entrance to an underground bar. After making her way in, she passed a few hours watching the television coverage of the tragedy that was unfolding around her. In due course, she was able to return to the apartment she had been staying in with her friend and contact her husband in England. Fortunately, her friend was safe. She had been taken on board a fire engine when they had become separated.

When she shared her experience with me, I felt privileged to have the opportunity to support her. Eventually, we managed to extinguish most of her symptoms. She was an extremely well-balanced person in a stable, supportive relationship and was able to put her experience into perspective and reclaim her life.

In 2002, I began studying again to obtain a supervisor's accreditation from BACP, so that I could supervise other counsellors. I had gained a great deal of knowledge and felt that the next step in my career was to become a supervisor. In my role as a supervisor, I mentor counsellors at various stages of training and have supported a number of them through to receiving their accreditation. Whatever level of expertise a counsellor or therapist has, it is always beneficial to discuss their clients with a supervisor. I gained my accreditation in 2004 to supervise both individuals and groups.

A CHANCE TO GET AWAY

My mother-in-law's health continued to deteriorate, and Henry spent many hours each day in the nursing home. Henry's mother died in January 2002, aged 99.9 years old. It took Henry a long time to get used to her death, as he had been spending at least three hours with her daily. All of a sudden, there was a big gap in his life.

I hoped that, after an appropriate mourning period, we could catch up on a lot of travelling that we had always talked about as being an option but had never found the time to think about seriously. It also might help him to clear his mind of his recent loss. Many couples plan a few trips abroad when their children leave home and they find themselves in a position where they have the freedom to think only of themselves, a freedom that is sweet and particularly well-deserved. Henry wasn't as keen on the idea as I was and said that he didn't want to take me away from my counselling. I reassured him that my work was flexible because of the nature of its short term contracts. I also made him aware of how excited I was by the idea of exploring an interesting place we hadn't previously been to. I truly thought it would be wonderful. We could build up some great memories for us to cherish at a time when we might not be in a position, physically, to travel so far afield.

At the time, there were four arguments against going. The first was that we already had many happy memories of travelling and didn't need to add anymore. We had visited America on two occasions to spend time with my family, had enjoyed various short term breaks to various parts of France, had been on two holidays to the Canary Islands and, of course, had returned to Kassel. With our business, we had also been lucky to visit many parts of the UK. The second was that we couldn't leave our house alone for more than a week or ten days in case of burglary. The third was that our youngest son Lee had started his own Web-based business and Henry was giving him some support and felt that he couldn't let him down. The final reason I have already mentioned: my work as a counsellor.

In my view, all of the reasons were easy enough to counter. In truth, Henry was comfortable at home and wished to keep things as they were. I ended up frustrated and reacted in a way characteristic of me, by getting more involved in my practice, my hobbies and nagging. Poor Henry!

THE SILVER SURFER

As I had been using a computer since 1984, when it became possible to go online, I asked my son to set me up, as, after all, he had taken a computer science degree. For me it was very important to familiarise myself with the World Wide Web, as I felt that it was a useful way for older people to keep in touch with the world, especially if they were unable to get out and about. When I joined the online community, there weren't that many silver surfers out there. Many of my friends were reluctant to acquire these new skills. I am aware that in the past ten years this has changed considerably, but I still sometimes come across people who refuse to adapt and have cut themselves off from such a large part of modern life. I absolutely love the fact that I can research anything online and can speak to family and friends on the other side of the globe via Skype. Four years ago I fulfilled my desire to set up my own website, which I designed with the help of a friend who works in IT.

Changes in technology have always fascinated me. Four weeks ago I bought and iPad. A few days later, I decided that I needed to purchase an iPhone as I am so accustomed to living with the constant support of this technology. How could I possibly manage without one? When I look back to my beginnings, when 99.9% of the population didn't even own a telephone in their home, I marvel at the wonders and ubiquity of all the technology that most of us take for granted. When my family first had a phone in Crouch End, I was unbelievably self-conscious about using it. My brothers and sisters made fun of me because I spoke in a "posh voice" whenever I used the phone. This left me phone phobic for years and years.

At school in the 1930s, we used slate tablets with chalk to work out our sums. Eventually, we moved onto paper and pencil, then ink pens with nibs and inkwells to dip them in, with the only way of getting the ink off your fingers being to rub them with pumice stones. It's funny how things change. Now I use an iPad instead of a slate tablet. Back then, the height of ambition for a schoolchild was to own their own Parker fountain pen. These days children carry around all kinds of gadgets. In the 1950s, BIC Biro pens were all the rage. Now you can go into Poundland and buy twelve pens, "Made in China", for £1.

In some ways, I think that my generation has been incredibly lucky. We have been privileged to witness so many technological changes in our lifetime, the kind we could never have imagined possible as children. The idea that one could be connected to the rest of the world whilst staying at home, even lying in bed, would have been ridiculed. On a personal level, I am delighted to have been around to master many of these marvellous inventions.

Obviously, the downside of this is the glut of information that invades our homes and consciousness. I can't help but feel that there will be some drawback in all this for those who are growing up in a world dominated by this technological luxury. As I see it, the main disadvantage is a loss of inner silence. Our younger generations are losing the ability to tune into their own thoughts and enjoy the simple pleasure of being in the present. As children we had to make up our own games. If I think back to my childhood, I can pinpoint thousands of moments where me and my friends or siblings had to make the most of what we had, making games out of our natural surroundings. I imagine children in the twenty-first century don't stimulate this creative, playful part of their brains to the same level as we did when they sit for hours in front of a screen playing computer games.

LONDON TERROR

I continued to go to a variety of seminars on a regular basis, as there is always some other area of human behaviour that can be explored or viewed from a different perspective. I attended a number of seminars offered by the BASRT (British Association of Sexual and Relational Therapy), as a number of my clients were presenting with internet porn addiction, and I wanted to learn more about the effect this could have both on an individual and on a couple's relationship. The first two in the series had been on offer locally, but the next one was taking place in London, near Kings

Cross, on the 21st July. This was in 2005, two weeks after the 7/7 terrorist attacks on the London Underground and transport system.

When I discussed going up to attend the seminar with Henry, he said that it was my choice. I responded by saying that I had lived in London during the Blitz and the IRA bombings and had no intention of living in fear. The only allowance I made was that I wouldn't go on the underground system, but would take a taxi to the destination of the talk.

When I arrived at Paddington, I was pleasantly surprised that the taxi cab service had been organised to deal with the increase in demand. They had introduced a system where particular destinations were sectioned off so that everyone who wanted to go to Knightsbridge, for example, would wait together in a designated queue and share a taxi, significantly reducing the cost and waiting time of the journey. I wanted to get to Kings Cross so joined the group of people headed in that direction.

I found the seminar highly informative. We looked at deviant and fetishist behaviours, its causes and how to work with clients presenting such issues. When we finished viewing a video related to various types of bondage, it was suggested that we break for lunch. On our return, the lecturer announced that there had been a terror-related incident in the local area, the scale of which she was unaware, and that we had a choice whether to stay for the rest of the seminar or to leave and try to make it home.

I decided that it would be more sensible to try and get back to Paddington, as the attack two weeks previously had left people stranded in London. I hailed a cab and asked the driver to take me to Paddington. He was quick to decline, saying, "Sorry love, but I am going back home!" I tried to hail another taxi; my efforts reaping little reward until one eventually stopped for me. The driver said that there was a lot of disruption and there would be quite a few detours. In the taxi, I was evaluating my chances of getting a train to Reading and decided that if it wasn't possible I could always walk to Chiswick, where my youngest son owned an apartment. I was very fortunate that the trains were running and jumped on a train back to Twyford, making it home safely.

I had been most concerned that Henry, hearing about another terrorist attack in Kings Cross, especially as he knew I was there for the seminar, would have been worrying all day. The amusing part for me was that, when he arrived home, he had no idea that this attack had even taken place as he had been in the warehouse all day and hadn't heard the news.

THE END OF AN ERA

For several years, I had been saying to Henry that we needed to downsize. At that stage of our lives, the upkeep of the house was taking too much time and effort, forcing us to lose out on valuable time that could have been spent on more enjoyable activities. I had begun to notice that the garden needed more tender loving care than either Henry or I had the time for. Although Henry continued to enjoy the gardening, it gave him aches and pains on his hands and wrists. The garden had simply become too large for us. All the trees had to be lopped again, and the pool was derelict.

I felt like I had a compelling argument for downsizing. It was inevitable that, eventually, one of us would be left alone. It was unfair to leave the burden of downsizing solely to the other partner. I have had many friends and family who have left it too late, with disastrous consequences. Being a very independent couple, we have always said that we didn't want our children to be burdened with looking after us.

I had spent the last seven years taking Henry to see newly-built houses in the area, as my reasoning was that a newly-built property would require less maintenance, something which would be important for us in our older years. We wouldn't have to worry so much about things going wrong.

We had also started to empty the loft at that time, sifting through forty-five years of things that had been stored up there once upon a time, just in case we might ever need any of it again. The process of emptying the loft was a journey down memory lane. Each new box would take us back to a time that lived on only through these objects and in our memories. It was like a time warp. We discovered an empty box within which our first TV had been packaged, even though the TV itself had long been given away or, perhaps, taken to the tip. The charity shops must have had a bumper time, as we donated cases full of blankets, eiderdowns, curtains, etc. We also found Ladybird books, loads of small toy cars, Scalectrix, railway stations, boxes of Lego bricks and a number of Action Man figurines.

The healthy part of the process was that it gave us the chance to make choices about what items we wished to retain and what to dispose of. This was much more preferable than having a house clearance firm arrive out of the blue and taking away any control we could have had over the situation.

There was an incident related to the clearing out of the loft that saddened me. I had been told about a wardrobe mistress involved with a youth theatre group in High Wycombe. She produced shows, usually musicals, twice a year during the school holidays. I donated a number of beautiful gowns, about twenty hats, just as many shoes and many other vintage items. I also donated one mink coat, with matching hat and jacket, as furs were now out of fashion. I handed these items over with good intentions, as she had told me that they also hired out these clothes to generate a little income for their productions. All I asked of her was that she would send me a couple of tickets to their next production. I never heard from her again, not even a thank-you note. Sometimes people disappoint me!

TV STARS

At the beginning of 2009, we were watching a favourite programme of ours on Channel 4, *Relocation, Relocation, Relocation*. The programme found homes for people who were looking to move. It was a cold February day and our house was typically chilly. As we watched the programme, I said to Henry, "I wonder whether we should contact them to help us find a house?" "If you like", he replied.

So I went onto the Channel 4 website and found an application form to fill in. On the site it stated that it might take several weeks before we received a reply. Much to our surprise, they contacted us within three days, saying that, in principle, they would be interested in using us for their show. The protocol was that they would come over to our house to ask some further questions and film us to see whether we would look alright and react appropriately.

So the adventure commenced. After signing a contract, a time was arranged when the presenters of the show, Kirsty and Phil, would come to our house to film. Going on the show proved to be very educational. We gained first-hand knowledge of what happens on the other side of the camera. In terms of practicalities, we were wired up for sound and there was strategic lighting, although we were not made up. I suppose this was to create a natural effect.

The first day was allocated as the "lifestyle" day, where they filmed us going about our everyday lives, which included me swimming in the pool at my health club and Henry gardening and playing his piano. On the subsequent two days, we went to view properties that they thought we might interest us. In total, the filming lasted four days. On the final day, we were filmed at various locations in Sonning village. Unfortunately, they were unable to find a suitable property for us, as Henry was finding the idea of leaving the house we had lived in for forty-nine years too difficult. Around the same time, we had considered moving into a small flat by the coast in Dorset and viewed three apartments there, two of which were great. But again, this fell through.

What the programme had achieved was convincing Henry that downsizing was a good idea. So we put the house on the market and found a buyer almost immediately. This wasn't a surprise. It was and I am sure it still is a perfect family home; however, for the two of us, especially for me, it had lost its charm. I was looking for something new, built with the latest labour-saving amenities that wouldn't need any maintenance in the foreseeable future. With ageing comes a greater anxiety when things go wrong. Again, my thoughts were: why should I inflict these types of concern on us at this stage of our lives?

Earlier this year, the company who made the original programme asked us if they could visit us to complete the story. In January, the company came by and filmed us in our new setting for its partner show, *Location, Location, Location*. I mentioned this book when they asked me what projects I was currently undertaking, and they included a short clip of me typing away on my computer in simulation of me writing this memoir.

The original show has since been repeated multiple times on the television, and both are available online at the Channel 4 website.

MOVING

Henry and I sold the house in 2010. At first, we thought about buying a new property but, instead of rushing into something, decided to rent an apartment virtually a stone's throw away from our old house while we kept up the search. We also thought it might be advantageous to see how we would react to apartment-living. I immediately enjoyed the simplicity of this kind of lifestyle.

Eventually, we found the perfect place. It was a newly built development, a combination of six houses and nine apartments all of different designs. We live in what is called a duplex apartment, named so because it contains two floors linked by a staircase. Our apartment is comfortably spacious with a downstairs lounge/dining room and large kitchen, as well two bedrooms upstairs with one en suite and a separate bathroom. There is plenty of room for Henry's baby grand piano. Outside we have the use of a communal garden and patio, which Henry enjoys pottering around in.

One of the great things about the complex is that the other residents are a wide variety of ages, including young professionals, a couple in their early sixties and a sixties widow. A couple of new babies have arrived since we have lived here. There is also a rich mixture of nationalities, including Mexican, Swiss, Brazilian and

Indian residents. We are the oldest couple but we feel just as much a part of the community as everybody else. It is a joy for us that, instead of being in a retirement community, we are living in an environment where we are surrounded by people from all the different stages of life.

We have a health club on our doorstep, which we use every morning. Through one of my clients, I heard of the latest keep-fit craze, Zumba. It seems that in the past ten years this type of exercise, originating in Brazil, has gone global. I thought I would try it for myself as I have always enjoyed Latin American rhythms. To my delight, despite being a fairly energetic dance workout, I have managed to master the various routines. I love the happy atmosphere in the class and truly feel the benefits until the next class. Again, I am the oldest participant but must admit that, when the music starts, I feel like a twenty-five-year-old again. In fact, I think I am somewhat addicted to this type of exercise. I have always enjoyed dancing, and these rhythms certainly take me back to my youth.

My "Stitched Up" group meets at a location that is only a five-minute drive and many of my friends from the group live in the vicinity. We have a bus that stops outside the development three times an hour to go into Maidenhead town centre. There is a main-line station to London within a ten-minute walking distance, but the best thing of all is that my hair dresser, who has cut my hair for nearly fifteen years, is just down the road. Previously I had to drive ten miles to visit him. Henry is twenty minutes closer to his favourite hobby, helping our son with his business. We are also close to the river for lovely walks, as well as many other green spaces.

After living here for a number of months, Henry believes the move was the right one for us, and I wholeheartedly agree with him.

EPILOGUE

I like to think that like a good wine I have matured with age, but that like the grape I have had to survive my fair share of frosty moments.

It is 2012, the Olympic Year and…

…**Still here**.

A few years ago, as I was driving into Reading on a bright, beautiful day, a funeral procession came into view. It was most impressive. There was a man in a top hat walking ahead, directing two black horses that were conveying the deceased in a fine black and glass hearse. This was followed by a large cortege of cars transporting the bereaved. The procession was headed toward Caversham Crematorium. As the road is quite narrow there, with on-road parking, I sat and waited along with the other traffic for the cortege to pass. As I sat there, with the car radio tuned to my favourite station, Classic FM, I heard the *Emperor Waltz* being played. At that moment, with the sincerest respect and solemnity, I thought: "What a great send-off! This is exactly the kind of thing I would like to have organised to celebrate my life." The sun was shining; the sky was an invitingly clear blue. My mind was flooded with images of couples whirling around in a large ballroom, with glittering chandeliers; the women dressed in sumptuous ball gowns with jewels glistening from their ears and neck.

Unfortunately, funerals are a lot more sombre in the Jewish religion. The ceremony consists mainly of prayers and readings from the Old Testament. There are no heartfelt speeches, erudite eulogies or any kind of celebration of the person's life. It is all so sad and serious. In recent years, I have been to a few Christian funerals and have admired the relatively celebratory mood, which is maintained despite the fact that there is sadness at the loss of a loved one. The tradition of family members and close friends speaking about their cherished and most personal memories of the deceased always provides me with a warm feeling, because, as long as those who have passed away are remembered, they stay with us in our hearts.

So, here we are at the end of my memoir. My story has now been told. For the most part, the process has been an overwhelmingly cathartic experience for me, yet, at times, quite difficult and painful. It has helped me come to terms with my own mortality and given me the platform to reflect upon the future, however long mine may last.

Passing into the current decade, I am surprised to find the world awakening to a terrible period of global anxiety. There is too much unrest in the world; too much aggression, violence and insecurity.

After enjoying almost three decades of economic growth, the West is heading toward severe economic insecurity. The current decade plays out amidst a global financial crisis that has brought back austerity measures reminiscent of how things were when I first arrived in the UK. In major cities around the world, people took to the streets as part of the Occupy movement to protest against financial inequality. In the UK, in 2011, many young people marched on London to carry out largely peaceful protests against a hike in university tuition fees. In August of the same summer, many cities across the country were targeted by more violent groups of young rioters who caused mass disruption and damage by looting shops and setting fire to buildings and cars.

In many North African countries, notably in Tunisia in 2010 and in Libya, Egypt and Syria in 2011 and 2012, socio-economic unrest sparked full-scale political revolution. This became known as the Arab Spring and saw long-standing regimes overthrown in clashes of bloody violence, amidst mass human rights violations.

The balance of power, wealth and productivity is now based in China, India and Brazil etc. In the West, we are confronted with unemployment, uncertainty and banking chaos. This unrest has touched me deeply. In truth, I have never felt as insecure as I do today.

Between 1913 and 1919, my father worked in Holland, where he had a small business making Cuban cigars. He spent this whole time saving in order to be in a position to get married when he returned to Germany. In 1919, following the war, his savings became as worthless as paper during the inflation of the 1920s. In the present, with the uncertainties in the financial markets, I fear that I might have to deal with something similar. I am sometimes haunted by existential fears that history will repeat itself and our life savings will be taken away from us after working towards them for nearly sixty years.

It also reminds me of something my mother used to say about the Yellow Peril during the 1930s. She used to say that in the future, which we can now think of as our present, the Chinese would take over the world. During the years that Henry and I travelled all over the UK, I would frequently joke about this with him whenever we came across another Chinese restaurant.

Having spent many months looking back and writing about my life, I think that it has also made me aware that for every bad day there is a good day. What's more is that in every good day there are bad moments and, likewise, in every bad day there are good moments.

In completing my story, I have found myself continuously questioning what it is that drives me. I keep asking: why do I keep pushing myself to venture down so many unfamiliar streets? Similarly, why was I unable to accept that I should, or could, have settled down in my sixties and enjoyed a more relaxed lifestyle, spending my remaining days going on leisurely outings, spoiling myself with long indulgent lunches or joining a bowling club? The answer is quite simple. I still have an ambition and conviction to explore and to learn. I feel the need to be involved in the world in some way, regardless of it having significance. I just love sharing my energy, which seems to generate relentlessly from a place deep inside me that I don't understand. All I know is that, as my life has progressed, this energy has helped me make some great choices.

The most fulfilling part of my life has been the past twenty-two years, since I made the decision to become a counsellor and began studying psychotherapy. I have seen thousands of clients, having specialised in working with people who can be described as healthy people reacting to life events. Working mainly in short sessions has meant that I touch these strangers' lives for as little as six hours, and yet, in that short time, our time together can be life changing. I have always been interested in people, so it has been rare that I ever find it difficult to connect to a new client. It is also part of the reason I have received so many positive testimonials from clients indicating that my time with them has worked wonders.

I have learnt that, as individuals, we are all unique, distinctively moulded by our experiences of family life in our early years; also that our reactions to certain life events will be the same whatever gender, race or culture we are born into. From working with both individuals and couples, I understand that men and women are, indeed, different in terms of their perception of life, their friendship circles and their resilience in the face of adversity, amongst other things. Although, as the ageing process continues, there appears to be some kind of crossover stage, where women become stronger and more resilient and men appear to get in touch with their creative, more feminine side.

There is no doubt that as we grow older, there are many things that get harder, many of which are chemical, biological and inescapable. This has been as true for me as it has for everyone else that has ever lived; although I feel like I have been able to deal with many of these inevitabilities by keeping my mind stimulated and my body active, passing each milestone of ageing with reasonable comfort.

What is the meaning of (my) life? What has it all been about up till now? Have I achieved enough? Have I left my mark? At some point everyone asks themselves these ultimately unanswerable questions. I feel that, essentially, life is about change. Change is the only constant in life. The more adaptable we are, the easier it is for us to see change as a challenge rather than a threat. I feel like this needs to be repeated:

"Change is the only constant in life. The more adaptable we are, the easier it is for us to see change as a challenge rather than a threat" – Me, Margot Harris

A few years ago I read about a group of women in Florida, who called themselves WITS, Wise Women in Training. I would like to identify myself with them. The older I have become, the more wisdom I have acquired. Rather than stemming from the classroom, my education now comes from a myriad of sources. I continue to learn from my love of books, from the wonderful World Wide Web, from my loving husband, my lovely friends and family, and from the wide variety of my clients' life experiences. I feel privileged that so many people have trusted me to share so much of their lives over the years and that they continue to do so.

I will end with my favourite quote, from the world renowned social scientist, Robert R. Carkhuff, PhD.

"In the end, what matters is how we end our lives. If we die growing, then we validate the attempts of others to do likewise. We pass on the legacy of life:- That the only reason to live is to grow! If we do not live and die growing, then it is as if we were never here at all for ourselves and others." – Robert R. Carkhuff, PHD

In Jewish celebrations we use a toast, "L'Chaim", meaning "to Life". So, regardless of which vintage you are: "L'chaim".

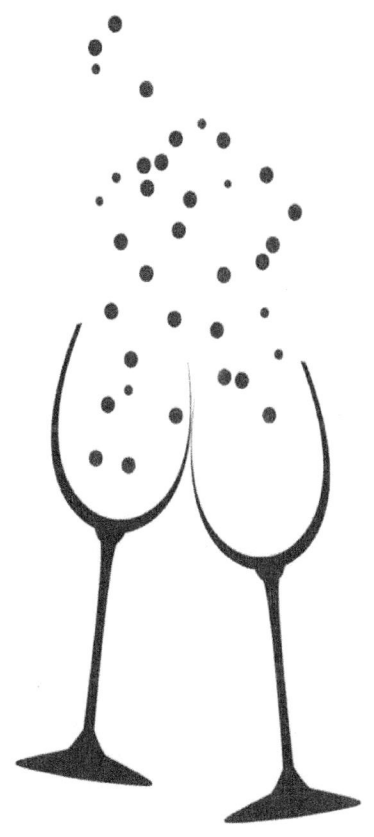

Printed in Great Britain
by Amazon

77471544R00088